Foreign Travelers in America
1810–1935

Foreign Travelers in America
1810–1935

Advisory Editors:

Arthur M. Schlesinger, Jr.
Eugene P. Moehring

UNCLE SAM AT HOME

James Howard Bridge

(Harold Brydges)

ARNO PRESS
A New York Times Company
New York—1974

Reprint Edition 1974 by Arno Press Inc.

Reprinted from a copy in the State Historical
  Society of Wisconsin Library

FOREIGN TRAVELERS IN AMERICA, 1810-1935
ISBN for complete set: 0-405-05440-8
See last pages of this volume for titles.

Manufactured in the United States of America

∽⌣ιↄↄ∽

Library of Congress Cataloging in Publication Data

Bridge, James Howard, 1858-1935.
    Uncle Sam at home.

    (Foreign travelers in America, 1810-1935)
    Reprint of the ed. published by Holt,
    New York
1.   United States--Social life and customs--
1865-1918. 2. National characteristics,
American.
I. Title. II. Series.
E168.B83   917.3'03'8   73-13153
ISBN 0-405-05446-7

UNCLE SAM AT HOME

BY

HAROLD BRYDGES.

NEW YORK
HENRY HOLT AND COMPANY
1888

DRUMMOND & NEU,
Electrotypers,
New York.

TROW'S
PRINTING AND BOOKBINDING COMPANY,
NEW YORK.

CONTENTS.

UNCLE SAM AT HOME.

CHAPTER I.

WHERE HE LIVES.

"Map me no maps, sir; my head is a map—a map of the whole world."—FIELDING.

I'VE heard that you have a fence round England to keep people from falling overboard during the night," said one of Uncle Sam's boys to me, with that exasperating deliberation with which the family is wont to administer a take-down. I had been dilating on the grandeurs of the British Empire, "whose morning drumbeat, following the sun and keeping company with the hours, circles the earth in one continuous and unbroken strain of martial airs," whose argosies crowd every port, and whose flag, unfurled in a hundred lands, is everywhere the symbol of constitutional liberty. As I swelled with patriotic pride, this was the pin with which the representative of the biggest nation on earth pricked me.

It is anomalous that in caricatures Uncle Sam is invariably represented as lean and gaunt, while John Bull appears as a stout, burly giant. For Sam delights in bulk. He is nothing if he is not big. The biggest waterfall and the greatest showman on earth are his;

and great is his delight therein. He is proud to have had the greatest fires, and the biggest swindles. The greatest war, the longest railroad, the highest statue, the largest rivers, the biggest herds of swine, the highest tariff and the biggest piles of grain—all are classified under one head. Bulk is the measure of superiority; and as Uncle Sam has the biggest things in creation, he has no superior.

Of course he has the biggest continent. There is no falling overboard there. Hear, ye peoples of the diminutive states of Europe! hear a native orator descant on its wondrous size and beauty!

"The grandest empires of the whole world, of ancient or of modern times, sink to petty provinces beside its vast dimensions. The whole possessions of Rome, when her golden eagles spread their wings victorious from the burning sands of Africa to the

mist-clad hills of Caledonia, fell short of the immensity of our new-world domain. Russia, vastest of modern sovereignties, could be lost in our half-hemisphere, beyond the power of all the detectives in Christendom to find her. France, land of Napoleon, at the tread of whose legions but little more than a half-century ago all Europe trembled as if taken with a Wabash valley ague, would scarcely overlap the single territory of Dakota; while Great Britain, whose morning drum-beat sounds around the globe, would hardly make a fly-speck on the face of Texas or California.

Do other lands boast of their great rivers? We could take up all their Niles and Thameses, their yellow Tibers, castled Rhines and beautiful blue Danubes, by their little ends, and empty them into our majestic Mississippis and Missouris, Amazons, Saskatchewans and De la Platas, without making rise enough to lift an In-

diana flat-boat off a sandbar. Do they brag of their seas and lakes?
We could spill all their puny Caspians and Azovs, their Dead Seas,
Nyanzas and Maggiores, into our mighty Superiors, Michigans,
Eries and Ontarios, and scarce produce a ripple on their pebbled
brims to wash away the eighteen-inch 'footprints on the sands
of time' left by the fairy-like slipper of a St. Louis or Chicago
girl. Do they prate of their romantic scenery? We have a thousand jewel-like lakes that would make all their vaunted Comos,
Genevas and Killarneys hide their faces in a veil of friendly fog.
The thunder of our Niagara drowns out the feeble murmur of
all their cataracts, while the awful crags and canyons of our Yo-
semite and Yellowstone, the prismatic glitter and dash of our St.
Anthonys and Minnehahas, and the lonely grandeur of our hori-
zon-fenced prairies, boundless oceans of billowy verdure, dwarf
to insipidity the most famous scenes of Switzerland and Italy,
eclipse the wonders and glories of the Arabian Nights, and defy
all the skill of poet's pen and artist's pencil to depict the veriest
atom of their sublimity and their loveliness. Do they prattle
about their Ætnas and Vesuviuses? With our noses turning
somersets of ineffable contempt clear over our heads, we thunder
forth our Cotopaxis, Popocatapetls, Chimborazos and a score of
other jawbreakers whose very names alone are too huge for common
tongues—(I am aware that some of the specimens of national pro-
digiousness that I have mentioned do not just exactly belong to us
yet; but they belong to our next-door neighbors who are not as
strong as we are, and to our gloriously expansive Yankee spirit,
where or what is the difference?) Do other lands and nations talk
of their mines of jewels and gold? We answer with the exhaustless
bonanzas of California, Colorado, Dakota and New Mexico, where
mountains of gold and silver ore challenge the skies, and where
the ceaseless thunder of the world's greatest bullion mills resounds
in the yet warm lair of the Rocky Mountain grizzly bear. Do
they rave of the harvest fields of Germany and Britain, and the
vine-clad hills of France? We show them half a hemisphere with
soils and climates as varied as the tastes of men, and with capacities for production as boundless as the needs of men; yielding
everything cereal, vegetable, animal, textile and mineral, agricultural, horticultural, geological, zoological, pomological, piscatorial
and ornithological, ovine, bovine, capricornine, equine and asinine—

(the last including most of our alleged statesmen)—that all the wants of all the races, tribes, kindreds and tongues of earth can ever require. The sun in heaven, in all its grand rounds since 'the evening and the morning were the first day,' never looked down upon a more magnificent domain—a fresh and glorious half-world, grand in all its proportions and endlessly diversified, rich and gorgeous in all its adornments, resting like a vast emerald breast-pin upon the bosom of the four great oceans. It is the broadest land ever given to any people, the grandest and most beautiful, the most varied in its productions, and the most unlimited in its capabilities and its future."

And responsive to this burst of true Yankee eloquence, the peoples of the earth are flying in their thousands to seize on all this ungarnered wealth. The gaunt New Englander, the long-headed Scotchman, the prognathous Irishman, the fat-paunched Briton, the sanguine Spaniard, the patient Chinee, the heavy-footed Dutchman, with a brace of Cherokees are all pictured rushing wildly westward, to gaze on the 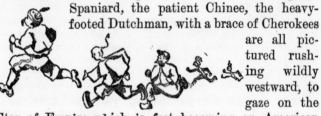 Star of Empire which is fast becoming an American " institootion."

A story is told of a number of Americans who, dining together in Paris, were dissatisfied with the patriotic toast as usually given—" The United States, bounded on the north by Canada, on the south by the Gulf of Mexico, on the east by the great Atlantic, and on the west by the broad Pacific." As an amendment one of them suggested " The United States, bounded on the north by the North Pole, on the south by the Antarctic Ocean, on the east by the Gulf Stream, and on the west

by the illimitable ocean." Even that did not satisfy
one of the party—a gentleman from Duluth. Said he
grandiloquently, "I propose as toast The United States,
bounded on the north by the aurora borealis, on the
south by infinite space, on the east by the precession of
the equinoxes, and on the west by the day of judgment."
The toast was drunk with an enthusiasm that rolled
across the Atlantic, and spread over the broad face of
Uncle Sam like a genial grin. He does like big things,
does this avuncular relative!

Exaggeration aside, the American continent is not
only a marvel of immensity, but of wealth and beauty.
None but habitual travellers and those who have lived
long in America can form any conception of its size, and
the majority of Americans are ignorant of its vast mineral treasures and its magnificent scenery. The single
State of Texas is as large as England, France and Germany combined. Into California, England and three
other European kingdoms could be placed side by
side and not overlap. Colorado, which in England
is hardly known except in connection with the Colorado
beetle, has nevertheless an area of 104,000 square miles
—nearly twice the area of Turkey, which has cost Europe so many millions of treasure and hundreds of
thousands of men slain. New Mexico, Dakota, Arizona
and Montana are almost *terræ incognitæ* in Europe;
and yet they have a total area of 531,000 square miles,
which gives an average larger than Austria, and a total
equal to Great Britain and Ireland, France, Italy, Portugal, Greece, Denmark, Belgium and Holland.

The distances between cities on this vast continent
seem incredible when placed in juxtaposition with
European distances. The journey from New York to

San Francisco, for example, is three times as long as that from London to Gibraltar—is, indeed, five hundred miles greater than from England to Quebec. Rome is as near to London as Chicago is to Boston. Madeira is 170 miles nearer to Portsmouth than New Orleans is to New York; while Jerusalem is nearer to Kensington Gardens than Salt Lake City is to Boston Common. Buda-Pesth, Warsaw, Stockholm, are not quite as far from the British metropolis as Milwaukee is from Albany; and Madrid is 150 miles nearer. The Londoner is separated from St. Petersburg by a less distance than is the Philadelphian from Kansas City; and he might go to Cairo, and thence by Tunis and Algiers to Morocco, without traversing a distance as great as that from the Hudson to the Sacramento. General Sherman recently stated that the northern line of defences during the civil war exceeded five thousand miles. This would make a line as great as one drawn from London across the channel to Paris and Vienna, through Constantinople, Asia Minor and Persia to Afghanistan, on through the Punjab and away down central India nearly to Madras. Look up your geography, friend! You will hardly understand such a statement without a map.

I once heard Mr. Lawrence Barrett say that he had crossed the Continent in three days and a half. For long runs without stoppage and good time the trip is unparalleled in the history of railway travel. The average run per day was equal to the distance between London and Naples. From New York to Pittsburgh, 444 miles, across the Allegheny Mountains, and round curves that would appal a Frenchman, there was not a single stoppage. Passing one station on the 3300 miles of line, the train was five minutes behind time; at other

places *twenty seconds* was the greatest deviation from
schedule time. A single engine conveyed the train 800
miles! And all this was across mountains of such
height and down grades so steep that travellers breakfast in the Sierras with twenty feet of snow around
them; four hours later they find wheat four inches high;
and the next day see pear and peach trees in bloom.

The great extent of American waterways is well illustrated by the following extract from a speech of Henry
Clay, one of a past generation of great statesmen and
orators of the New World:

"'Sir,' said the custom-house officer at Leghorn,
'your papers are forged! There is no such place in the
world! Your vessel must be confiscated!' The trembling captain laid before the officer a map of the United
States, directed him to the Gulf of Mexico, pointing out
the mouth of the Mississippi, led him a thousand miles
up it to the mouth of the Ohio, and thence another
thousand to Pittsburgh. 'There, sir, is the port whence
my vessel cleared out.' The astonished officer, before
he saw the map, would as soon have believed that this
ship had been navigated from the moon."

In early days, before the railways extended their arms
of steel into every corner of the land, the voyage mentioned by Henry Clay was a common one ; and many a
good ship has sailed twice two thousand miles before
reaching salt water. Nowadays ships for inland navigation are not generally constructed for ocean-sailing ;
and freight is transhipped at sea-ports into sea-going
vessels. But thirty years ago ships which had crossed
the Atlantic sailed through the great lakes, and dis-
charged their cargoes a thousand miles inland. And in
a few years great ships will pass through the deep canal

which is to join Lake Erie to the Ohio, and thence by the Mississippi into the Gulf of Mexico—a total sailing on fresh water of over five thousand miles. The river banks east of the Rocky Mountains are said to exceed 80,000 miles, counting no stream less than a hundred miles in length ; while the whole of Europe has but 34,000 miles. The Mississippi system alone affords 35,000 miles of navigation !

Distance, as such, has lost all meaning in America. The New Yorker does not say it is 1120 miles to Burlington, Iowa, but 30 hours ; not 913 miles to Chicago, but 24 hours. This circumstance is very striking to a European, who is constantly puzzled when asking distances by being told " six hours," or " only a day." When Uncle Sam visits Europe he retains for a time the same mode of reckoning distances, and after achieving the nine hundred miles between London and Rome as he would the trip to Chicago, perhaps congratulates himself that he has " done" the Continent. A few such trips, however, teach him that Rouen, Paris, Geneva, Genoa, Venice and Florence, with all their wealth of association and historic interest, lie on the route ; and then he takes a more leisurely course. Distance is now not even reckoned by the hours required to traverse it : it is simply ignored. And this is why the American on the Continent impresses other travellers as affectedly despising European distances. At home he thinks nothing of several days' journey. He has probably crossed more than once to the Pacific—equal to a trip from England to the Gold Coast. It is only ninety hours to Denver— not two thousand miles. remember. So great is Uncle Sam's indifference to distance that he is beginning to regard Japan as a mere suburb of America, as he has long regarded Cuba and Brazil.

Herbert Spencer says that the Veddahs of Ceylon, a wild tribe without religion or any social bonds, are so simple and honest that when theft was described to them they did not understand it. "Why should a man take what is not his?" they asked with a bland innocence that implied little contact with Christian Europeans. Uncle Sam is equally at a loss to understand the kleptomania which European nations display in respect of other people's territory. The international skurry for annexation which is ever going on, in the Pacific, in Africa, and in Indo-China, is totally incomprehensible to Uncle Sam. Cuba, Mexico, Panama, the Sandwich Islands, have all offered tempting baits in vain. Says he, "Our farm is already too big for fencing stuff;" and with a shrug he leaves the struggle to Britons, Germans and Frenchmen. What a blessed thing it is to know when one has enough! The mother-country might here learn something from her child.

Uncle Sam has at home the biggest store of minerals that Nature ever lavished on man. His coal field is as large as Great Britain and France combined, and constitutes about three fourths of the world's supply. Yet he used last year only two thirds as much as John Bull did. John is getting behind in some things, but he keeps ahead in this. In Nevada a gold and silver mine has been yielding a king's ransom every year since 1860. And some years it would have been a more important king than any I know of—except, perhaps, the late Victor Emmanuel—who would have been worth so great a ransom. In 1876, for instance, this Comstock lode yielded £2,600,000 of gold and over £4,000,000 of silver! A single copper mine near Lake Superior has twice produced nearly ten thousand tons of ingot copper

in one year. The ore is
so rich in that region that
masses of almost pure
metal are found in all
sizes up to several tons.
The Indians made weap-
ons of it without smelt-
ing. Iron is found in every State, and it is worked in
twenty-two ! Yet here, again, England keeps ahead, pro-
ducing in 1885 nearly twice as much as America. But
Uncle Sam is "hurrying up," as he says. He has
nearly doubled his yearly product since 1871; and he is
offering wagers to the world to beat every competitor
before 1890.

"And the rocks poured me out rivers of oil," says our
father's brother Samuel, quoting Scripture, as is his
wont when talking "manifest destiny." The rocks of
Pennsylvania pour out seventy thousand barrels of oil
every day ! The oil is pumped in pipes from the wells
to the seaboard, a distance of three hundred miles.

Then Nature, as if she could not do enough for our
transatlantic uncle, has given him wells of natural gas
—gas distilled in the bowels of the earth, and rushing
to the surface with a pressure of nine hundred pounds
to the square inch, so that engines are sometimes
worked by direct pressure. At one well near Pittsburgh the daily yield of gas is thirty million cubic feet
—enough to supply half London or the whole of Paris.
Seven such wells would supply the whole of the United
Kingdom. Shades of Watt and Humphry Davy !
Would that we had such wonders in our own little
island ! We would show the world that our manufactures, so advantaged, needed no "protection" — no

coddling legislation. But Uncle Sam is weak, and requires the baby's walking-chair which he has had so long, and which has grown with his growth. Without it he thinks he would fall. Maybe he would, poor gentleman ! Crutches are not calculated to develop stout legs.

Such is Uncle Sam's home—such the goodly heritage that has fallen to our father's brother. When George the Madman threatened, and the Hanoverian lion howled, Uncle Sam stood on Bunker Hill, boldly delivering himself of homilies on the rights of men by musket and reaping-hook. At Lexington he fought the battle of Britons in England. He deserved something good. He has got it; and we rejoice with him in his good fortune.

CHAPTER II.

UNCLE SAM'S BOYS.

"Traffic's thy god, and thy god confound thee."—*Timon of Athens.*

T Christmastide, in the year 1620, a babe was born into the family of nations, destined to preach peace and good-will to men in a new voice. No flourish of trumpets sounded its advent; no glittering ceremonial marked its coming. Its cradle was as rude as that which sixteen hundred years before held the Babe who first preached peace, personal liberty, and the identity of human interests the world over. On the 22d of December, 1620, the *Mayflower*, a ship of 180 tons burden, landed her living cargo on the desolate shores of Massachusetts. Weary and worn with a long voyage, anxious about the future, impeded with sickly women and children, the Puritan pilgrims bravely stepped into a new and unknown world, trustful in God, and full of faith in themselves. Looking back through the mists of two centuries and a half, we cannot realize the desolation of their position. In the midst of a northern winter, infinitely more severe than anything experienced in England, surrounded by savages of unknown character, and with nothing before them but the gaunt bare trees of the forest and the reach of sandy shore, along which the wind swept with dirge-like wailing, their condition almost makes us weep. To us the picture is a glorified one, as we look down the grooves of time at the handful of men, standing with bare heads that wintry day, offering to the All-father thanks for safe arrival and for liberty to worship Him in their own way. Surely had "God sifted a whole nation that He might send grain over into this wilderness."

It is these brave and hardy sons of liberty who have given backbone to the American character. From them is derived the "grit," the energy, the enterprise of the American character. The spirit which was undaunted in presence of the wilderness, the savage, and wild beast during that northern winter, has come down to descendants, and has even permeated the whole American people, diverse as is their origin as individuals. A typical example of American endurance and courage—a credit to his British ancestry—is Stanley, "the man who found Livingstone." Another noble type—a worthy follower of Franklin and Ross—is Lieutenant Greely, commander of the ill-fated expedition to the Arctic regions. In Commander Schley's book we get a narrative, simple and pathetic, which recalls Livingstone's struggle with death, alone in Central African swamps, kneeling in prayer at his camp-bed:

"Lieutenant Greely was the first man in the desolate camp at Cape Sabine to hear the steam-whistle of the *Thetis*. He told his companions that he had heard a steamer's whistle, but they thought it was only the roaring of the wind. Sergeant Long went out of the tent, but speedily returned with the remark that there was nothing in sight. Lieutenant Greely settled himself in his sleeping-bag, but was aroused not long afterward when Lieutenant Colwell cut down the tent. 'Greely, is this you?' the gallant rescuer asked. 'Yes,' said Greely in a faint, broken voice, hesitating and shuffling with his words. 'Yes—seven of us left—here we are—dying—like men. Did what I came to do—beat the best record.' Then he fell back exhausted. Lieutenant Greely, dying like a man, but proud of his exploit, and conscious that he had beaten the best record, is a noble type of American grit."

In the attack upon Vicksburg it was needful to transport troops through the bristling batteries of that Gibraltar of the Mississippi. The regular crews of the transport steamers refused the hazardous service; and General Grant called for volunteers. So eagerly did the soldiers respond that the commander had to cast lots among the crowds who offered themselves; and one Illinois boy, who had drawn the coveted privilege of exposing his life, was offered a hundred dollars in greenbacks for his chance. He refused the money, and held his post.

These are the men who, in two hundred and fifty years, have subjugated a continent, cleared its forests, pierced its mountains, bridged its rivers, and built a network of railways and canals to aid communication between their thousand wealthy cities. And proud should England be to claim them as her children. It is a noble progeny. Pity that the mother and child do not understand each other better.

But admirable as is American grit, it is one of those good things of which we can have too much. It developed during the severest struggle with nature that man has ever undertaken. The original struggle has long since ceased, and now men are wrestling with each other.

I know of several great traders and corporations who have deliberately tried to crush out every one whose business competes with their own; and two brothers in New York, both wealthy, revile each other publicly: they are business rivals! So fierce is the competition, so intense the pressure, that it is no uncommon thing to see a young man's hair tinged with gray. I know one whose hair was slightly silvered before he was old enough to have a beard. Yet there is no need for all this commercial wrestling. Everybody who can and will work is well off. Poverty is unknown except among those who are so shiftless that they would be poor and miserable in Paradise. The root of the evil is the desire of personal aggrandizement. Every man's efforts are directed to his own well-being or that of his own family. Selfishness is supreme. As Dudley Warner aptly puts it, all are "actively engaged in acquiring each other's property;" and the sight is not an edifying one. If half the mental effort and energy spent in trying to circumvent commercial rivals were bestowed on public affairs, Uncle Sam would not only have the most perfect form of government, but the best working political system in the world. And no one knows better than he the difference between these two.

Genuine Yankees such as are portrayed on the stage and in comic journals are growing scarce. Most persons have never seen one, and believe that the quaint angular figures, drawling nasal tones, and odd conceits ascribed to them are the products of the brains of novelists and playwrights. Nevertheless they do exist, and a writer in *Harper's Bazar* lately described one whom he met at Santiago de Cuba. The city is a very strange one. The houses and shops are so built that the walls can be almost entirely thrown open, while the interiors have courts that are unroofed and unobstructed to the sky. The money of the country is strange, and nothing about the city is familiar to an American. The Yankee had just landed when he spoke as follows: "Somehaow I can't tell when I'm indoors and when I'm aout. I've got a room, *or somethin'*, in a hotel here, and I've been into it, quandarying araound, but I could not tell when I was in the parlor or when I was in the kitchen or back yard, *so I'm standin' aout here in the park not to make any mistake.* I started daown the street a minute ago, but I got afraid I might make a mistake and git arrested for bein' found in somebody's back parlor. I've got a lot of the money of the place, but I can't make heads nor tails of it. I took some of it back whar I got it, and passed it over the same counter—so I reckon it's genuine. I could write the history of the place already. All I need is the dates. It was evidently built the year after the flood; it's been shook down by an earthquake, burned up by a volcano, resettled, and left just as 'twas found. The whole country is best whar it's been let alone. Wherever the people have touched it they've made a mess of it."

I myself have met one or two specimens of the old Jonathan type, and I have envied them their powers of expression. For originality of metaphor, quaint phrases, rough eloquence, and a manner at once ludicrous and dignified, they are incomparable. One of them speaking of a disrespectful hotel-clerk—a type now happily extinct—said "he oughter be sot straddle on an iceberg and shot through with a streak of lightning!" I gave this delicious morsel to a stolid Yankee from the land of wooden nutmegs, expecting at least a smile. But never a ripple crossed his face as he slowly drawled: "Rather rough on the clerk."

Another Yankee fresh from the country and surprised to find a homely dish in a Washington hotel, exclaimed as he sank his fork into a chicken croquette: "Gosh! hash!" If brevity is the soul of wit, the American is the funniest man alive!

In England the term Yankee is thought to be slightly disparaging—an idea which we probably got from Confederate sympathizers during the war. Another mistake we make is to apply the name to all Americans. The people of the Southern States call all Northerners, both east and west, "Yankees," but they disclaim the name themselves. The people of the Western States call only those living in the Eastern States, or east of the Hudson River, "Yankees," and these are the only people who acknowledge the name, and always so describe themselves. A southern planter having business in Boston, asked his daughter what kind of present he should bring her back. "Oh, a Yankee dude 'll do!" she replied with a laugh.

In these days of national self-glorification it may not be out of place to recall the origin of the name Yankee. When the Pilgrim Fathers landed on Plymouth Rock the friendly Indians asked of what people they were, to which they replied, "English." But the red man could not pronounce the word, and "Yengeese" was as near as he could get to it. The transition from Yengeese to Yankees was easy. So that the proudest name of the proudest section of the American people is only a variation of "English"!

The ideal American is tall and gaunt, with prominent features, high cheek-bones, and bright sparkling eyes. The ideal Englishman is one with ruddy round face, rotund figure, and a genial smile of contentment at things as they are—at least at home. It is not difficult to see how these ideals have arisen. The gaunt, nervous type of Englishman in whom the Celt predominates —Prof. Tyndall is a perfect example—is the one whose enterprise and restlessness have often taken him from home and planted him in a transatlantic environment. The ruddy sanguine Saxon is he who remains at home, a contented honest old Tory, satisfied with his condition as yeoman or squire, and too rooted to his beloved land to think of migration. But the one is as much an English type as the other, though our national peculiarities result from a union of the two characters. It is the sanguine temperament that gives stability to our institutions and solidity to our works. It is the quality that makes ours

> " A land of old and just renown,
> Where freedom slowly broadens down
> From precedent to precedent."

And it is from the nervous type that the American derives his dominant characteristics—the restlessness and discontent which prompt search for new and better methods, as of old they gave rise to political and religious dissent. This type of Briton is the same the world over; but because it is more common in America, we have got into the habit of speaking of energy and enterprise as traits peculiarly American. Yet Englishmen have lost none of those qualities which gave to the world the steam-engine, the railway, the steamboat, the telegraph; that first lighted our streets and homes with gas; that created new breeds of horses and cattle; that taught the world gravitation and evolution; that in-

vented Bessemer steel, the steam printing-machine, the
spinning-jenny, and power loom; that originated clearing-
houses, insurance systems, Lloyds, and the penny-post;
that discovered the circulation of the blood, and the
value of vaccination; that gave the world trial by jury,
and habeas corpus acts; and under Cromwell led the nations to democracy and free institutions. Englishmen
are still great in enterprise and energy. They have made
railways for all Europe, and are now doing the same for
Mexico and China. They make roads in South America,
and harbours in Siam. Their superabundant energy runs
over into foreign investments to the extent of six hundred millions sterling. And to energy and enterprise, they
add a quality that is none the less admirable—thoroughness. It is this which gives to English work, whether
in the Andes or in Fiji, that solidity so eloquent of per-
manence, which has become a national characteristic.

The greeting that Uncle Sam gives you is not of that
clammy solemnity which the French say comes from our
damp climate, and which gives you a forlorn feeling that
you are only a unit among a thousand millions—a mere
speck in the universe. He takes your hand in a hearty
grip, calls you by name, and inquires after your health
with a tenderness approaching anxiety, and so encour-
ages you in the belief that your existence is a matter
of interest outside your own family. Sam's friendliness
and familiarity make you "feel good," as he himself
says. It is not the least admirable trait in his character.
For there is no earthly reason why two particles of
humanity which chance has brought together for a moment, should spend that moment in revolving around
each other without contact, each solicitous about the

Whence and Whither of the other. That they find themselves in the same corner of the universe ought to be a sufficient basis of sympathy. Our common humanity is the ground on which Sam says "Come on!" and John says "Keep off!"

The expression "common humanity" here reminds me of that very common humanity on the Pacific coast, the heathen Chinee. And I would add in the most emphatic way, that it is not Uncle Sam who in this case says "Keep off!" It is that product of our British civilization, the Irish emigrant, whose vote has a value to the professional politician not easily stated in words. Kearneyism is the local name of the Anti-Chinee movement.

The ingenuity which Uncle Sam's boys display in "acquiring each other's property," shows itself in many curious forms. In advertising, ingenuity rises to the level of genius. Never for a moment is the tourist allowed to forget that he has a liver, or a stomach, or chilblains. The very rocks proclaim the value of Skunk's Seaweed Bitters, and Hygeia Water. At Niagara, while your attention is divided between the mighty flood and a pestering hackman, the moss-covered bank at your feet invites you to try Blank's Little Liver Pills or Smudge's Kidney Invigorator. Every fence as you dart along the railroad or glide down the river extols the virtues of Gargle Oil. Even Liberty herself has been in danger; for an enterprising quack offered to build

Project for enlightening the world

the pedestal in consideration of the privilege of paint-
ing the Statue with his advertisements. But even
Yankee enterprise refused to sanction the desecration.
A summer excursionist lately wrote to the *Chicago Current* that in looking over the side of his canoe, he espied
a snapping-turtle at the bottom of the lake, and on its

horny back was
painted the adver-
tisement "Gents'
Ready-made Cloth-
ing marked down
Low."
The annexed cu-
riosities are from
advertisements of western graziers' cattle-brands.

Here is another curiosity:

B EAUTY FADES, like Broadway $5 suits. Cameron sells
all-wool ones for $5. 202 Flatbush ave.

C OME YE WHO LABOR and are heavy laden and get a
complete suit at Cameron's for $2.50.

C LEOPATRA'S HISTORICAL beauty is nothing compared
to Cameron's $20 nobby all-wool check suits for $8. 202
Flatbush ave., Brooklyn.

D ROP DEAD'S indestructible $8 corduroy suits are just the
thing for country romping, $2 to $4.

G IVE to the poor and you lend to the Lord. Diagonal pants,
50c.; wool ones, $1, at Cameron's.

J ONAH'S PREDICAMENT in the whale was nothing compared to the feelings of clothiers who pass Drop Dead's and
see the business he's doing now.

K ING HUMBERT works from 6 A.M. to 12 P.M. Cameron
never sleeps, studying how to give customers $2 for $1.
202 Flatbush ave., Brooklyn.

M ONEY is the root of all evil; 98c. of the root will buy a de-
sirable $2.50 child's suit at Drop Dead's.

O VER the hills to the poor-house is the way Broadway clothiers lead. Cameron leads to prosperity.

P ALMA HOUSE, 92 Bowery—50 men wanted; rooms 25c.
per night; all modern improvements.

P UT MONEY IN THY PURSE and get a $60 satin-lined
suit for $20 from Drop Dead, Brooklyn.

P YRAMIDS OF EGYPT are commonplace to the all-wool
youths' suits at Drop Dead's for $2.50.

W HAT'S THE MATTER with your hands? It's the dye
from a New York $5 suit. Why, I got one from Drop
Dead for $2.50, and it don't fade like that."

In the windows of city bar-rooms the eye of the
stranger is frequently caught by the announcement
"Free Hot Lunch, all day." If he enters he will probably be invited to take a bowl of soup or chowder—soup
made of fish or clams—while temptingly displayed along
the counter are bread and cheese, ham, sardines, pickles,
corned beef, perhaps pickled oysters. I have seen
twenty different dishes so displayed, including the costly
caviar; and the guest is at liberty to help himself to any
or all. This is another kind of advertisement. The
San Francisco free lunch is really a first-class repast;
and is in great favor. I have seen it stated that the
free lunches served in the saloons of New York cost
nearly twelve million dollars a year. It would be interesting to know how the estimate was obtained.

Here is an example of American ingenuity in another
line, copied from a Pittsburgh paper:

"DALTON, GA., Jan. 1.—Edward Pickens and Jennie Allen
eloped on Wednesday night. They had no license, and the bride
was under age, but these difficulties were surmounted by the

pastor, Silas Jasper, who had been requested to perform the ceremony. At his suggestion the party went to a point where the counties of Gilmer, Gordon and Murray join, and with each party standing in a different county and the preacher astraddle of a county line the ceremony was performed. The question now is which county has jurisdiction of the case."

I read a short time ago in a Florida paper of a local judge who, being arrested and locked up while intoxicated, called for pen and paper when he got sober, and issued a writ of habeas corpus directing the sheriff of the county to bring the body of himself before himself as a judge; and on the perplexed officer's refusal to obey the mandate, fined him for contempt of court. If the sheriff had had the usual humour of Uncle Sam's boys, he would have refused to pay the fine, so that he might commit himself in default to his own prison. In this way he might have amused his district by a judicial complication as funny as that which Gilbert's Lord Chancellor outlined in *Iolanth*.

This ingenious judge reminds me of another judge who "got badly left" by an ingenious negro. The following is the story, told in the quaint language of one of the actors:

" As we got into South Carolina we were joined by a judge from Pittsburgh. I forget just what court he was judge of, but he had been travelling South for his health, and had just figured up that he had paid out twenty-five dollars in fees to waiters, and was mad all the way through. He vowed by his baldness that he wouldn't pay out another red cent, and we encouraged him as hard as we could. When we went up to the hotel the landlord gave us a big room with three beds in it. A big negro brought the trunks up, and when he was ready to go the judge called to him and began: ' Colored person, stand up ! Now I want to say to you that I shall expect prompt service without fees. You have brought up my trunk; that's all right—it was your business to. I shall want water, and I may want a fire, and I shall probably ask you to go of errands, but if you even look fees at me I'll throw you out of the window!' We were there two days, and the waiter was vigilant, humble and willing; but as we made ready to depart the morning of the third, in comes a constable with a warrant to arrest the judge for threats of personal violence. It had been sworn out before a justice ten miles away, and the complainant was the first negro waiter. It took the two of us to hold the judge down on his back during his paroxysm, and when he had cooled off a little the negro slipped into the room and said: ' White man, stand up! Now I want to say to you dat a five-dollar bill will settle dis yer case jist as I feel now, but if you goes to callin' names, or pullin' hair, or kickin', I'll stick fur twenty five dollars! Dat justice am my own brudder, and he's jist achin' to send some white man ter jail fur six months!' We sat on the judge again for about twenty minutes, at the end of which time he handed over the amount and was pronounced sane."

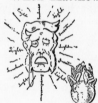

When Matthew Arnold first visited America, to shed on Uncle Sam a benign effulgence of sweetness and light, his hyper-sensitive soul was often vexed by the Philistinism which is inevitably associated with great material development. Here is a bill of fare which is said to have caused the sage so much pain "on board" a Western train:

CHICAGO & ALTON R. R.

TRAIN LUNCH.

BILL OF FARE.

" Tho' we eat little flesh and drink no wine,
    Yet, let's be merry; we'll have tea and toast,
    Custards for supper and endless host
    Of sandwiches and jellies and mince pies
    And other such ladylike luxuries.—*Shelley.*

COFFEE, WITH CREAM, ... 10c.
    " Coffee which makes the politician wise,
    And see thro' all things with his half-shut eyes."—*Pope.*

Rolls, ... 10c.
    " Hot or cold, white or brown, but all as sweet
    And dainty as you'd surely wish to meet."

Ham Sandwich, ... 10c.
    " An essay, a taste of heaven below."—*Waller.*

Tongue Sandwich, ... 10c.
    " The delight of old and young."—*Swift, An Echo.*

Pie, ... 10c.
    " Who'll dare deny the truth: there's poetry in pie?"—*Longfellow.*

Milk, per Glass, ... 5c.
    " He drank of the milk foaming fresh from the cow."—*T. D. English.*

> " Serenely full, the epicure would say,
>   ' Fate cannot harm me, I have lunched to-day ' "
>   —*Sydney Smith.*

Hard-working and ingenious boys are the sons of Uncle Sam. Less work and more play is what they want: not so ingenious but more ingenuous, they would make better citizens and happier fathers and husbands. It is a trait of undeveloped races that they are incapable of prolonged effort, especially when the reward is remote. In America men seem to have been overdeveloped, and to have gone to the opposite extreme. Their application is unceasing. The savage works only when the reward is visible and immediate: the American works even after he has secured the object of his labour. It is unfortunate that it is not the custom in America, as it is in England, for a business man to retire after attaining a competency. This would make room for other men, and reduce competition.  But in America if a man makes a fortune in one business, he often goes into something else, and aims at success in that. Americans are beginning to regard mere commercial success as the standard of a man's value to his country, forgetful

that under conditions of such keen competition as now
prevail one man's success often means another man's
failure.

There is still a good deal of quiet satire indulged in
by Uncle Sam's boys when they speak to an Englishman
about the Revolution. At the Centennial Exhibition
the occasion lent itself to this kind of humour, and, without abating their characteristic politeness and hospitality, the Americans made it slightly uncomfortable for
some Englishmen who remain sensitive on the subject
of British prestige. I have just been reminded of this
by re-reading in Fischel's *English Constitution* that,
despite the king's intention, the war was brought to a
close by " a resolution of the Commons, March 4, 1782,
declaring that ' all those who should advise the con-
tinuance of the American war were to be treated as
enemies to the king and country.' " I quote this ancient
item to help to rectify the confusion which still exists
in the minds of some of Uncle Sam's boys concerning
the popularity of this war.

At the completion of the Statue of Liberty there was
a good deal of talk about the brotherhood of men in
general and republicans in particular;
and some very acute Yankees exemplified,
as their grandfathers had done before
them, that it is easy for Uncle Sam to
mistake French Anglophobia for love of
the abstractions—liberty, fraternity and
equality. The mistake is excusable, for
the French constantly make it themselves. At the time when Franklin was being fêted
in Paris, and Lafayette was fighting the battles of enslaved Americans, the condition of Frenchmen living

under Frenchmen was infinitely more degraded than that of the Boston men who threw the tea overboard. The Bastile still stood, the symbol of despotism; and the sound of the cheers that greeted the American representatives passed through its barred windows to the unjudged captives within. Outside the city, peasants dared not weed their crops for fear of disturbing the young partridges; while limitations were imposed upon the use of manures, lest the flavour of the game killed and eaten by nobles should be injuriously affected. A hundred and fifty years after Cromwell, French workers were forced into the marshes at night, to beat the frogs into silence, because the lady of the seigneur was ill; and the great lord sold to the wretched peasant permission to crush his handful of wheat between two stones! If charity begins at home, what a golden opportunity was missed by Lafayette and the other young noblemen of France, when they undertook to vindicate the rights of man against hereditary despotism on American soil instead of in their own loved land!

The Americans were lately told that they ought to be for ever truly grateful that they are essentially British. This is like saying that an orange ought to be for ever truly grateful that it is not essentially a cocoanut. Of course Americans are of English stock; but no one is to thank for that any more than any one is to thank that we are not all Chinese or Bosjemans. No one could have made it differently. If the Americans had not been of English origin, they would not have been Americans. Their country might have been filled with Mexicans, Greasers, French half-breeds, but not with Americans,—Yankees, as we call them, with all the high qualities which the name connotes—the inherited love

3

of freedom, energy, enterprise and ability of the English, intensified by a new environment. Contrast the
devout, sturdy, independent Puritans with the first
colonists from Spain and France, whose only legacy to
America is a degenerate race of half-breeds. Compare
Quaker Penn's treatment of the Indians with the treatment which has exterminated the ancient Mexicans and
Peruvians, and destroyed their high civilization. The
difference in character shown by the contrast is the
difference between the grandsons of Englishmen in the
United States and the men who might have occupied
their place. And it is this difference that has made
America. To be grateful that New York and San Francisco are not the squalid camps of French and Spanish
half-breeds, is like being thankful that the laws of
gravitation are as they are, and that men, when they
slip, fall down and do not fall up, into infinite space!

CHAPTER III.

THE FAMILY GIRLS, WITH A DISQUISITION ON THE AMERICAN BONNET.

" Thou living ray of intellectual fire."—FALCONER.

S Boston City is the undisputed hub of the universe, so the Boston girl is the unquestioned centre of every female virtue, attraction and accomplishment. This sounds like an axiom, and it is one. The Boston girl shines in the social firmament as Venus in summer skies. Her brilliancy gives a shadow to everything it falls upon. Other stars, even those of first magnitude, wax faint and dim when she sheds her pure white light on mankind. America has much to be thankful for, but for nothing so much as for the Boston girl.

The Boston girl is as peculiar to the Hub as is Bunker Hill or Beacon Street. She is the product of an intellectual atmosphere so rare that ordinary girls wilt and wither in it, and become strong-minded female suffragists with corkscrew curls and goloshes. She is the brightest and prettiest creature that ever bathed in the sunlight of knowledge. She is a very humming-bird in beauty, a dove in gentleness, an owl in wisdom,

A very humming-bird in beauty.

and a swallow in physical motion. She is—but let me specify:

All studies, from ecclesiastical history to the theory and practice of the banjo, come within her range. Equally expert at composing a bonnet or a sonnet, she is likewise at ease when discoursing on the morals of the ancient Huns or the domestic habits of the Bosjemans. Biology, Psychology, Sociology come to her as naturally as Huyler's candy and coquetry to other girls. In the giddy whirl of the dance she will look up into your face with a soul-entrancing gaze that is peculiarly

Bostonian, and whisper: " What do you regard as the
real bases of Schopenhauer's ethics?" You softly con-
vey to her the desired information; while the fragrant
odours from her breastplate of flowers float up and
make you feel that Mahomet was inspired when he
made houris in green silk the attraction to Paradise.
" What do you consider the best test of the authenticity
of a Mexican *chalchihuitls?*" Again you respond; and
so throughout the dance. Under the charm of the
Boston girl the waltz becomes an intellectual exercise,
and the polka the intercommunion of sympathetic
souls.

Lest the reader should think my faint eulogy of the
Boston girl overdone praise, I beg to quote the testimony of an observant writer who says:

" I sat between a couple of them the other night at that same
symphony concert, and came home in a sort of daze as to how
any two creatures could know so much about so many things and
carry it all off so easily under that graceful garb of simplicity and
unaffectedness which fits the Boston girl as if it were made to
order. They knew the special style of every man in the orchestra,
from the leader, Listemann, to dear, departed Lichtenburg, of
happy memory; they could tell if the oboe fell a sixteenth part of
a half tone from the pitch, or if the furthest kettledrum was
snared an infinitesimal atom too tightly. When the andantino of a
Tschaikowsky concerto was fainting away in a strain of delicious
sweetness that you or I would as soon think of analyzing as an
echo from Paradise, it reminded one of ' that staccato study of
Rubenstein;' when the andante *con fuoco* began it recalled to the
other something of Brahms. They discussed the relative merits
of the Lang school and the rival clique with a discriminating
justice that would not have shamed Solomon; they gossiped in
German and translated the French song on the programme; they
spoke of one woman's back hair as ' a study,' and another
woman's bonnet as ' a daisy,' so that they were human after all.

They knew the genealogy of every one in the hall, which is another essentially Boston accomplishment; and I found out in
the pauses for intermission and breath that they hammered brass
work, wrote essays, painted in oil, read Wagner's music at sight,
went to the theatre every other evening, kept up an intimate
acquaintance with five hundred friends, and had their own ideas

on the subject of housekeeping. And
yet, I give you my word of honor,
they looked as pretty and as artless
and as quiet as if they had not
two thoughts in their two heads;
and, although they whispered a great
deal, they managed to do it without
disturbing any one but myself, who
rather enjoyed it. For, thank Heaven,
their voices were free from the usual
American shrillness. You think, perhaps, that I have been
sketching an isolated type? My dear friend, my style is as
plenty as peas on the Fourth of July."

Yet withal, the Boston girl is so modest of her intellectuality that she has been known to put paper covers
on her Balzac, Lessing or Kant, in the originals, and
ostentatiously label them "Called Back"!

When the telephone joined Chicago to New York,
the first words that passed along the wire were: "Is it
true that Chicago girls have big feet?" A pause.
Then, sad and low came the answer: "Alas, it is!"
And so it is, if journalists' statements, reiterated a
thousand times a week, are to be trusted. But journalists' statements are not to be trusted—in America.
Newspaper writers there have been classified by one of
themselves into liars on space, and liars on salary. As
a matter of fact, Chicago girls have not big feet.
Neither have the girls of St. Louis, though every liar

on space and time from Babylon to Yazoo City says

they have. The reader will remember that even that spread-eagle orator quoted in the first chapter could not resist the temptation to allude to "the eighteen - inch 'footprints on the sands of time' left by the fairy-like slipper of a St. Louis or Chicago girl." Gentle reader, this is an exaggeration. The fairy-slipper incases a fairy foot, and that supports a fairy form. For all American girls, whether Bostonians, Chicagoans or St. Louisians, hailing from the Monumental City or from Oshkosh, are bright, pretty and graceful, without pedal deformity or abnormal digits.

I have sometimes thought that American men are unable to appreciate the glorious girls of the Republic. Engrossed in business pursuits, ever engaged in the mad race which has for prize the omnipotent greenback, the average American man is intellectually the inferior of the average American woman. Of course he is quick and clever at his business. That is as needful to his survival as fleetness is to a deer which lives where beasts of prey abound. But in the gentle arts which make up the brightness of life, the American man is generally inferior to his sister or his wife. She can chat with you about anything, from the exorbitant charges of the English tailor in New York to the evidences of the nebular hypothesis; and this with a

piquancy that is irresistibly attractive to a Briton.
At the Tower of London a small cannon is shown which
was taken at Bunker Hill. A party of Americans were
looking at the gun while a sergeant related its history.
" Yes," said a lady, "you've got the cannon, but I guess
we've got the hill." As a patriotic epigram this would
be hard to beat even by a Boston girl. The brother or
husband will "talk shop" if you understand it, or
express a strong opinion on the last unnavigable addition to the American navy. But in art, music, literature, he is conspicuously deficient. This is probably a
reason why journalists delight to ridicule the Boston
girl: male readers buy the paper and laugh at the absurd
intellectuality of women. As these same women are to
be the mothers of future American men, we may confi-
dently hope that the next generation will not despise
mental activity in females, and may even encourage it in
men. President Cleveland's sister, contemplating some
such ideal, exclaims: "What a world of enjoyment and
improvement would spring up! How Athenian would

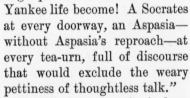

Yankee life become! A Socrates
at every doorway, an Aspasia—
without Aspasia's reproach—at
every tea-urn, full of discourse
that would exclude the weary
pettiness of thoughtless talk."

Notice that Aspasia is here
the ideal—not Xantippe. The
virago, indeed, has little scope
for development in a land where
a divorce can be promptly obtained, without scandal or
publicity, for incompatibility of temper, or "for such
other causes as the court in its discretion may deem
sufficient."

So much has been said of the Boston girl that the reader may not unnaturally conclude that the Hub is not only the centre of female intellectuality, but the periphery as well. This, however, is not the case. Mental activity is filling the gap in women's lives made by the commercial engrossment of men; and this extends from Massachusetts to California. Indeed, as one moves westward, one finds men's mania for dollars ever growing more frantic. It is an admirable trait in American women which leads them to fill lonely hours with worthy pursuits. Indianapolis is thought of by English people as being in the backwoods, far from civilization. Even by eastern Americans it is looked down upon, and the inhabitants slightingly spoken of as Hoosiers. Here are the heads of a few subjects discussed in the session of 1885–1886 at the Indianapolis Woman's Club:

Our Southern Stories and Story tellers, by May Louise Ship; A Symposium on the Puritans—In Literature, by Elizabeth Cleland; In Politics, by Arabella C. Peelle; In Social Life, by Janet Douglass Moores;—John Milton, by Margaret V. Marshall; A Study of Paradise Lost, by Elbizaeth Nicholson; Conversation on the man Milton as shown in his Works, led by Catharine Merrill; Sir Christopher Wren and his Monument, by Margaretta Elder; The Cartoons of Raphael (illustrated), by Harriet McI. Foster; Cavalier Songs (illustrated), by Nannie I. Newcomer; Conversation on the Women of the Time—The Queen; the Princess; the Court Beauty; the Brave Wife; the Good Daughter; the Literary Woman;—The Stuarts as Authors, by Martha H. Bond; The Royal Society, by Flora McDonald Ketcham; Conversation on Literary Patronage, led by Sarah Wallace ; Wit and Wisdom of Fuller, by Eliza G. Wiley; Jeremy Taylor, by Amanda W. Wright ; "The Country Parson," by Kate R. Winters; Nature and Poetry, by Jennie T. Hendricks; The Decay of the Drama, by Eliza C. Bell; Conversation on Histrionic Art, led by Marie Louise Bright; Victor Hugo, by May Wright Sewall; Conversation, led by Helen B. Holman; "Comus Crowned," by Julia D. Butler; The Regicides and their Fate, by Mary Harrison McKee; Conversation on Superstition Now and Then, led by Mary Stewart Carey; Scottish Bards and Ballads, by Mary A. E. Woollen; Celtic Element in English Literature, by Ellen F. Thompson ; Conversation on National Characteristics of Wit; John Dryden, by Harriet Noble; Conversation on Consistence in Change, led by Mary E. N. Carey; George Elliot, by Mary A. McGregory; Conversation on Anonymity, led by Hannah G. Chapman.

De Tocqueville, speaking of Americans, said: "If I  were asked to what cause I think the singular prosperity and growing power of this people should be attributed, I should answer, 'To the superiority of their women.'"

The personal relations of men and women in America are in many respects unique. The sex is awarded great liberty from the earliest age, and this induces an independent bearing which is in attractive contrast with the timid, unreliant manner often seen in Europe. As a result, the men seem more chivalrous than those of any other nation—for chivalry is compatible only where the sex is allowed great freedom. A woman may travel alone from Maine to Mexico, not simply without molestation, but everywhere receiving acts of kindness from her male fellow-travellers. If she gets into a crowded street-car, some man invariably offers her his seat, while he rides for the rest of the way hanging on to the roof-straps, and bumping against the knees of the seated passengers at every curve and stoppage. The American excels as an indulgent husband—so I have been told by

English girls who have married Uncle Sam's boys. American women themselves are not unappreciative of the high quality of American husbands, though many silly girls are found willing to marry some European fitznoodle with a title. "Let me see, dear, what is Clara's fiancé baron of?" asks the proud prospective mother-in-law of a title. "Bar-ren of funds!" growls paterfamilias, who had to supply the *dot*.

This *dot*, by the way, becomes an object of interest even to the governments of some European countries. If an American girl is unfortunate enough to fall in love with the uniform of a German or French officer, she must furnish a *dot* of ten or fifteen thousand dollars before she can marry it. And while she is doing this under the immediate direction of the European Minister of War, her family and home-surroundings in America become objects of dip-

It becomes hers.

lomatic interest to the Minister of Foreign Affairs. If the *dot* is forthcoming, and if investigation of the suppliant's family and personal history has revealed nothing to make her unworthy of the high honour she aspires to, the uniform is brought out, and after an appropriate ceremony it becomes hers. If she or her English cousin marries a Frenchman of any degree, she is liable to repudiation after a while—except she notifies her marriage to a French consul or some other government official of authority. These are facts which it would be well for the publishers of Baedecker and Murray to put into their guide-books. They are much more important to American girls than the circumference of the tower at Pisa or the height of the Trocadero.

A couple of years ago a professor in Vassar College stated that the number of pupils in the institution was little more than half what it was in 1875. "The trouble is," said he, "that Vassar has become a thing to poke fun at. Half the jokes about girls are put upon Vassar students. Their doings are ridiculed, exagger-

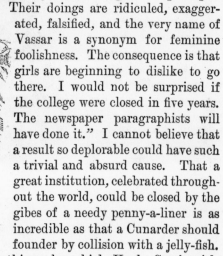

ated, falsified, and the very name of Vassar is a synonym for feminine foolishness. The consequence is that girls are beginning to dislike to go there. I would not be surprised if the college were closed in five years. The newspaper paragraphists will have done it." I cannot believe that a result so deplorable could have such a trivial and absurd cause. That a great institution, celebrated throughout the world, could be closed by the gibes of a needy penny-a-liner is as incredible as that a Cunarder should founder by collision with a jelly-fish.

A graceful pose.

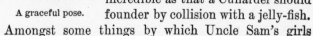

Amongst some things by which Uncle Sam's girls

show their good sense is a corsage which allows free
play to the lungs. Wasp-waists, the pride of many English girls, are conspicuously absent in America. The
result is a graceful pose and easy carriage altogether in-
compatible with tight-lacing. In this particular Fashion
would do well to cross the Atlantic eastward, instead of
to the west as she usually does. Curiously enough, an
American manufacturer advertises "Her Majesty's Cor-
sets." What are they?

But the English girl displays better sense in her
choice of boots. Broad soles and flat heels are in
favour with most of the daughters of Albion; while
American girls often affect the French *chaussure,*
with high curved
heels placed near the
middle of the sole,
and as little like the
human foot as a dress-
maker's model is like
the Venus de' Medici.
Still this fashion is
rapidly giving way to the English style. Two or three
years ago an American girl with comfortable-looking
boots was a rare sight; and the improvement has already
manifested itself in the increased exercise which Uncle
Sam's girls now take.

In several of the extensive valleys of California, where
the climate is equable and moist, there is rapidly developing a race which in appearance is an exact counterpart
of the English people. Ruddy complexions and ample
forms give the people the appearance of having lately
arrived from Kent or Sussex. If Uncle Sam's girls
generally added the fresh clear complexion of an Eng-

lish girl to their numerous other charms, there would be a stampede of men from Europe for wives. Only two things would then be wanting to make her at once fit for Paradise: a pair of wings and a softer voice. The Boston girl often has a voice of un-American sweetness. Her sisters in other towns invariably speak in such loud tones, that it takes a Briton a long time to get acclimatized.

Those who have been taught that American women are tall and gaunt, like the schoolmistress of amateur theatricals, will be surprised to find how many fine buxom matronly women there are in eastern cities. Indeed, Americans themselves are expressing surprise at the change—for such it is. A few years ago, I am told, American matrons looked as ill-fed as some of the care-worn business men look now; but at present they suffer no lack of that healthy adipose tissue which gives amplitude to the figure and geniality to the face. As the struggle with nature—or rather with each other—becomes less keen, we may expect similar changes in the physique of American men. The jolliest among them have already acquired a pleasing rotundity of figure. May their shadows never grow less!

As a bonnet is to the female mind the physical expression of every happy emotion, the embodiment of all poetry and beauty, the crystallized result of ages of sentiment, and the highest product of feminine ingenuity, I have left all mention of it to the last as the boy leaves the most savory morsel of his dinner—"that he may have a good taste in his mouth." Though a description of a bonnet is more difficult to write than the description of a battle, or an essay on Dolichocephalic Crania

and their owners, it is clear that any chapter on Uncle
Sam's girls would be incomplete without some notice of
their bonnets. For the American bonnet is of a very
unusual kind. In the first place it is bigger than its
European prototype. As the English hare has acquired
great size, strength and fleetness since its transportation to
Australia, so the European bonnet has advanced to perfection in America.
There it has reached
the acme of size
and of elaboration of
parts. It rises from
the curl-crowned
brow in majestic
height, a fitting cap-
ital to so glorious a
column. But its
greatness is not with-
out inconveniences.
"Madam, if you
would kindly remove
your hat, I should
be able to see the
stage," remarks a

The acme of size.

gentleman at the theatre to a young lady who is in front
of him. No reply. "Madam, I cannot see anything
at all on the stage." No reply. "Madam, if you don't
remove your hat, you'll be sorry." Still no reply. The
gentleman deliberately puts on his own hat—a heinous
offence in any room where ladies are. "Take off
that hat, take off that hat!" immediately resounds
through the theatre. The young lady, in great confusion, instantly removes her bonnet, and the gentle-

man behind her settles down complacently to enjoy the play.

Not only does the American bonnet excel in size: its shape is as varied as the feats of a contortionist. Spiral, circular, triangular, quadrangular, orbicular, cuneiform, fusiform, dendriform, curviform, polygonal, multilateral, elliptical, vaulted, hooked, conchoidal, heart-shaped, bell-shaped, pear-shaped, oblique, flat—every form to which there's a name, and many forms to which there are none, does this mystifying head-gear assume. Ribbons, flowers and feathers are arranged

over, round and under it in labyrinthic disorder. To a man it appears as confused as a sermon in a strange tongue; to a woman as coherent and orderly as the same sermon to a native. It is like one of those mysteries

At a Bonnet Show.

which, while puzzling half the world, the other half calls an "ism," and then thinks it knows all about it!

CHAPTER IV.

PATRICIANS AND PLEBEIANS.

" My shield is Or, sir, and the arms I bear
Three mushrooms rampant ; motto, Here we are."
                   THOROLD ROGERS.

 HE Republic of America is a vast hive of industry. Every honest man in the community is engaged in some gainful occupation. Such idlers as exist are of a very different type from those who in Europe eat up so large a share of the produce of the workers. The difference has been well indicated by an American lady, who was commiserated on the absence of an aristocratic class, " who have no occupation and go about from place to place enjoying themselves, you know!" " Oh," said she, " we have such persons, but in America they are called tramps."

Uncle Sam has the biggest farm and workshop in the world. His farm comprised in 1880, 837,628 square miles — an area greater than the United Kingdom, France, Germany, Austria, Hungary, Holland and Belgium collectively. This mighty farm is divided amongst four million of Uncle Sam's boys, giving an average of 134 acres to each. Its value is estimated at two billion

4

sterling. Its yearly produce is worth £1,106,270,000.
His grain-field, exclusive of cotton, tobacco and the

The American Aristocracy
(None other genuine).

like, is greater than
the whole of Spain,
or half as large
again as England,
Ireland and Scot-
land. His hay-field
covers an area as
large as Portugal
and Belgium; while
he gathers cotton
from plantations as
large as Holland.
How little some of
the kingdoms of Europe seem in the light of such a
contrast! His potato-fields, sugar-brakes and tobacco-
plantations would hide many of the old-world monarchies
beyond the power of their kings to find them again. A
great landowner is Uncle Sam!

Mulhall says that the farmers of Red River, Minnesota, can send their grain for 12*d*. a bushel to New York,
or 15*d*. to Liverpool (say 4700 miles); while the citizens
of Athens pay 36*d*. a bushel from Marathon, a distance of
only 15 miles.* The full importance of this fact is seen
only when placed by the side of another, also borrowed
from Mulhall: Nearly one third of the grain of the
world is grown in America! Truly the world would go
ahungered without America. Malthus did not take
the Republic into account when he made his famous
calculations.

---

* Balance sheet of the World, page 14.

With live-stock, too, the national farm is supplied in proportion to its great size. For every sheep, cow or horse in the United Kingdom Uncle Sam has ten. His twelve and a half million horses would make a double procession from America to Egypt. If his 48 million mules and asses, oxen and cows, joined the ranks, the procession would be equal to the journey from London to Sydney, thence across the Pacific to Valparaiso, and through South America to Rio. If the procession were augmented by his 45 million sheep and 57 million pigs, the ends would overlap after twice putting "a girdle round the earth."

Uncle Sam's workshop is on an equally gigantic scale. Sixty millions of people live within the limits of the United States, and a big workshop is required to keep them all supplied with boots, clothes, houses, furniture, railways, and all the other essentials to nineteenth-century happiness. England was the workshop of the world a few years ago, and headed the nations as a manufacturer. This honourable position she has had to resign to her precocious child. It is difficult to compare the relative positions of the two countries in this particular, because the American returns include as manufactures the products of the corn-mill, the slaughterhouse, and the forest. But the estimates of British manufactures as recorded in 1882 are nearly three hundred million sterling less than those of Uncle Sam in 1880. The number of workers in the census year was more than seventeen and a quarter millions, or 34·68 per cent of the whole population. That is, one person in every three, including women and children, was at some gainful work.

In America many kinds of work are open to women

which are closed to their sisters in Europe. The half-million women-workers in 1880 included nearly three  thousand barbers, three hundred journalists, seventy-five lawyers, two thousand four hundred physicians, one hundred and sixty-five preachers, and over three thousand printers. There are many signal-women and female detectives, and at least one female Mississippi pilot. But our dainty country bar-maids, and those magnificent creatures who with queenly dignity minister to thirsty Londoners, are equally unknown in America. Uncle Sam regards this form of female servitude as degrading as the field-work of French and German women.

When we remember that a century ago, the American continent was practically a *terra incognita* with the exception of a narrow strip along the Atlantic coast, the change seems almost miraculous. Who can estimate the work that has been required to change the wilderness into a populous continent, dotted over with cities, covered with a plexus of railways and canals, and displaying in every part the evidences of man's activity? The vast shipments of grain and cattle, the endless columns of statistics of manufactures, give no adequate idea of American industry. For this we must follow the progress of the country from its condition of savage wildness to its present advanced position as a leader of nations. In the building of great cities where forests lately stood, in the growth of farms where a few years ago wild beasts and wilder men engaged in a fierce struggle for existence, in the development of perfect political institutions, cemented in blood, and made strong and enduring by prolonged effort—such are the things which bear the most eloquent testimony to American industry. The American colonies had an industrial origin; they fought for industrial freedom; by industry they grew into a great nation; their consolidation was effected by labour, not by militancy. Work, not war, has ever been their watchword. By this have they attained a prosperity which the warlike nations of the Old World will strive for in vain, until their young men exchange the musket for the hammer, and drill in the workshop and forge instead of in camps and barrack yards.

Every European nation has passed through a stage in which it was held that war was the only honourable calling, and that work of every form was degrading. Our Norse forefathers, from whom we have inherited many of the traits that have given the choicest parts of the world to our English race, believed so thoroughly that fighting was man's proper business and that work was fit only for slaves and women, that they conceived heaven as a place where their time was to be passed in daily battles with magical healing of wounds, and hell a place for women and workers. And we see the influence of these and kindred sentiments in the contempt that has grown around many once-excellent words. "Villain," "churl," "boor," and "clown" were once the simple designation of peasants; and equivalents of two, "Kerl" and "Bauer," have survived dishonour in

Germany. " Clodhopper " and " groundling " further
testify to the degradation of that form of labour which
was not personal; while the elevation of " knight " and
" esquire " show how much more honourable were menial
services—those performed by the *moins né*. And not
only was labour despised: learning too was put under a
ban, and " crafty" and " cunning," once meaning
skilful and knowing, now connote deceit and strategy.
Even yet the business of war is held in highest esteem
in Europe; and though there are many estimable men
who cannot understand the pride with which Voltaire's
Frenchman declared, " *Mon métier est de tuer, et d'etre
tué,*" it is still to soldiers that public monuments are
ofterest erected. We continue moreover to invoke the
divine anger on the Queen's enemies with the same
Norse ferocity with which we invite the Lord to smite
his own enemies " on the hinder parts." There is surely
a good deal of the old ferocity in the modern North-
man's religion.

A London journal recently offered a prize for the
best list of the twelve greatest living men. Nearly
eighteen thousand voters considered General Wolseley
greater than John Bright or Prof. Huxley! Surely
we deserve the charge of eccentricity which other
nations make against us. And the really greatest
living man—the man who will leave the deepest personal impress on his age, who will live longest in the
hearts and minds of men of all nations, who has helped
mankind the furthest onward, *is not named at all*—
did not receive a thousand votes! And while Herbert
Spencer is thus ignored, Bismarck receives 32,245
votes, Moltke 13,968, and Churchill 13,117 ! !

A curious commentary on social gradations is suggested by Roget's *Thesaurus,* where "flunkey, jockey, cad, swineherd" are given as correlatives of "emperor, king, majesty," etc.   "Scullion, charwoman, gyp," are stated as the opposites of "empress, queen, princess," etc.   As the list proceeds with "hireling, parasite, mercenary, puppet," as correlatives of "duke, doge, seignior," one cannot help thinking that those who acquiesce in such a classification deserve it.   But I suppose most people will here claim to belong to "the middle class," which Roget leaves comfortably vague.

A friend, who I fear is more dogmatic than accurate, says that the patrician "Howard" is derived from "hog-ward"! If true, here's confusion for the Buggs! But how consoling to the mass of plebeians, who are derived from conditions of like humility! That a despised Saxon swineherd should be the forefather of a Howard of Effingham, while the product of a long line of kings may be a libertine Stuart or an imbecile George, is certainly encouraging to the plebs.

I wonder if any "old aristocrat," such as Thackeray describes in his Book of Snobs, "swelling with pride, the descendant of illustrious Norman robbers, whose blood has been pure for centuries, and who looks down upon common Englishmen as a free-born American does on a nigger"—I wonder if such a one ever had the curiosity to calculate how many ancestors he had, say six hundred years ago. If he did, the result must have astonished him. Everybody knows that we each have four grandparents, eight great-grandparents, sixteen great-great-grandparents, and so on for a few generations; but few probably have ascertained that this ratio taken back twenty-five generations gives each of us one hundred and thirty-three million ancestors—a rather startling result in view of the fact that twenty-five generations ago the entire population of England was probably not more than three million. Of course the calculation is fanciful, but not more so than the notions of blue blood and pure descent prevailing in aristocratic circles. At this day the blue blood of those who "came over with the Conqueror" must be millions of times diluted, and fortunate its possessors that it is so.

It is common to find in American novels such expressions as "great families," "best society," "long descended;" and we hear of the "exclusiveness" of the "fastidious American aristocracy," "who think as much of their positions as the haughtiest *veille noblesse* in Europe." "A patrician crush" is according to one writer the synonym of what another calls "a toney gathering." These crushes and gatherings have, however, little of the aristocratic element in their composition. They are for the most part but fashionable circles in which prevails the milliner's estimate of life. It is into this society that the young lady makes her

Her "Deb-bew."

"deb-bew," — as *début* is startlingly pronounced in America. In no other English-speaking community do the people stickle so for the titles "gentleman" and "lady." I was told by my Irish-American laundress that "the lady what did the clear-starchin' got twelve dollars a week." And I have heard of a cabman who asked: "Are you the man as wants a gentleman to drive him to the dépôt?" During an investigation concerning the Cambridge (Mass.) workhouse, one of the witnesses spoke of the "ladies' cell." And a newspaper reporter, writing of a funeral, had occasion to say how the "corpse of the dead lady" looked.

The plebeian who by dint of hard work has accumulated wealth, often aspires to patrician distinctions. Tiffany of New York is said to have a pattern book of crests, from which the embryo nobleman may choose a scutcheon emblematic either of his business or of some less worthy characteristic. A shirtmaker of Connecticut, having made a fortune by an improved cutting machine, announced his intention of getting a coat-of-arms. An unappreciative commoner asked him if the design would be a shirt rampant. "No," he gravely replied; "it will be a shirt pendant and a washerwoman rampant." This was possibly suggested by the attitude of the washerwomen who called upon the President to demand that the towels of the Treasury Department should be "laundried" by native talent and not by Chinamen. A successful dustman adopting a crest chose the motto  *Fidelis ad urnam,* which by a very free translation was made to read, "Faithful to the Ashes."

Byron said that families with long pedigrees are very much like growing potatoes: the best part of them is in the ground. This is one of those truths which are so self-evident after you have heard them, that you wonder you never thought of them before. In no country is this dictum so true as in America. The children of the successful merchant or manufacturer expect to begin life where their fathers ended. They are brought up extravagantly, in full knowledge of their fathers' wealth, and with no incentive to effort. But in a society which has no idlers these young men soon tire of their own company, and longing for a new sensation, enter business. There they have to compete with men who are working their way up, and in doing so have developed traits which the rich man's son sadly lacks. He " gets left," as the American phrase well describes a defeat, and pretty soon he proves the truth of the Byronic simile.

A good story is told of an old senator from Kentucky, a lover of those old-fashioned virtues that went along with " Jeffersonian simplicity," who delighted in snubbing the dude of his day. Meeting one of these one day in the street, he was accosted with " How d'y do, Senator? I called on you yesterday."

" Yes, I got your card. By the way, what was that horse's head on it for, and the letters?"

The youth laughed airily.

" The head, judge, is my crest—the steed which some of my ancestors rode to battle ; and the letters E. P. mean *en personne*—I left the card myself."

" Oh! I see," dryly replied the judge.

A day or two later they met again. "I got your card, judge, this morning. But what do those extraordinary figures on it mean?"

"Oh! the mule is *my* crest. I sell mules in Kentucky; and the letters S. B. A. D. mean that the card was sent by a darky."

I think it could be proved, if data were obtainable, that those who have the most right to these emblems of nobility are least mindful of them. In his thoughtful little book entitled "Old World Questions and New World Answers," Mr. Daniel Pidgeon relates that at Great Barrington, Connecticut, he was hospitably entertained by a widow, the mother of a female compositor, whose ancestral chart included William the Conqueror, Matilda of Scotland, Alfred the Great, Henry I. of England, Lewis the Fair, Charles the Bald of France, and Charlemagne and Hildegarde of Swabia, his wife. Remember, these are from the genealogy of a working-woman who still lives in an obscure town in New England. Mr. Pidgeon says: "The fervent desire of every New Englander is to trace his lineage to one among the handful of God-fearing and courageous men who first colonized America, and rarely seeks to lengthen his pedigree by research in England, content if he has sprung from the virtuous fathers of his own country." A desire of this kind is in the highest degree praiseworthy: it does not express itself in those ostentatious crests and emblazonments that seem to proclaim their owner better than his fellows.

Armorial bearings were originally the signs which warriors placed on their shields or habits, in order to be distinguished from enemies in battle. A genuine coat-of-arms, therefore, implies descent from some old-time barbarian. By negative evidence, the families without crests descend from the herd of retainers, or from the masses of workers. It is a curious survival of the barbaric instinct which causes men to prefer (where they have the choice, as in America) a descent from some feudal tyrant and murderer, as all those fellows were, rather than an ascent from an honest swineherd or serf. If in these days it is nobler to suffer wrong than to be an evil-doer, surely it must be more honourable to have had a wronged and suffering ancestor, than a barbarous tyrant, practising on his trembling dependents his horrible *droit de seigneur* and the like.

CHAPTER V.

THE ANGLOMANIAC; WITH A NOTE ON THE FUNCTIONS OF THE DUDE.

"Thou damned antipodes to common-sense!"—ROCHESTER.

F the visitor to New York will walk down Fifth Avenue any fine Sunday morning after church-time, he will see a crowd of fashionably-dressed young men standing under the portico of the Windsor Hotel, sucking wooden toothpicks, and watching the people as they come from church. Others may be seen at the windows of a certain club in Fifth Avenue which has often been mistaken for a boys' school. These young men are dudes, the American variety of the London masher. They belong to that large class which scoffers call Anglomaniacs. They do not live at the Windsor Hotel; they merely get their toothpicks there, and once in a while patronize the hotel bootblack, just to give countenance to their loafing in the halls and on the porch. It was probably the sight of some such exquisite that evoked from Fuller the trite remark : "Nature generally hangs out a sign of simplicity in the face of a fool."

The Dude is the Anglomaniac *par excellence.* He has

the cockney drawl which actors in America affect when representing an Englishman; and though he does not drop his *h*'s in the traditional British style, he walks with the Piccadilly swing or the Pall Mall glide, whichever happens to be the passing masher fashion. He takes his father's cuff, and wears it as a collar; and putting a pane of glass in his eye, ogles with true masher-stare the ladies who pass him in the street.

The Pall Mall glide.

His gaiters are imported, as are also his gloves and his hat. He affects the society of such scions of British nobility as are attainable; and boasts of his acquaintance with the Earl of Rottenville and

The " Masher-stare."

Lord Gumboyle. Every change of gait, attire or occupation of the masher is quickly imitated by the dude. *Life,* the American *Punch,* has made many a laugh at the dude's expense. According to this journal, the dude's representative in London not long since sent to his club-friend a cablegram which read:

"Dust-carts are all the style. Get one, and tell the dear boys."

Forthwith dust-carts became the rage in New York. The office of chief scavenger was besieged by a crowd of young men wearing loose trowsers and single eye-glasses, demanding corporation dust-carts. The com- missioner could not supply more than half the required number; but those of the disappointed dudes who could afford it bought private dust-carts and harnessed them to high-stepping horses, and had a tiger on the back of the cart with folded arms in the regulation Hyde Park style. The poorer dude bought  a wheelbarrow and shovel, or a dust-pan and brushes. *Life* says the craze was at its height when consterna- tion was produced in the ranks of the gilded youth by another cablegram:

"Mistake of telegrapher. Dog-carts fashionable, not dust-carts. Great laughter in Lon- don."

With amusing seriousness, *Life* adds that Fifth Avenue was then free of the dude for a month.

A philosophical contemplation of the dude, in the plenitude of his powers of dispersion, fills one with admiration at the economy of nature. Nothing is allowed to run to waste—not even a dude. His place in nature, like that of the mosquito, is unperceived by the common mind; but the philosopher sees that both dude and mosquito fulfil important functions. The mosquito nourishes itself at the expense of others: the dude nourishes others at the expense of himself. He is the rich man's son, who distributes his father's wealth, and sets it circulating in a health-giving current throughout society in general but amongst publicans and sinners in particular. The dude is a provision of nature against the prolonged accumulation of .great wealth in families. Owing to this bland-looking type, there is hardly a great fortune in the United States which has passed as a whole beyond the second generation. " In America," says an observant writer, " there are but three generations from shirt-sleeves to shirt-sleeves." While the dude does his appointed work so well, there is no danger of an Aristocracy of the Dollar in America. A territorial class such as we have in England is impossible where free laws allow wealth to pass from the hands of the idle and luxurious into the hands of the industrious and frugal.

Let us respect the dude, then. Though he appears a noodle whose only soul is that supplied by his tailor, his mission is of great importance to society, and he fulfils his task far better than might be expected from his vacant looks. The dude is really a benefactor to his race. All glory to the dude!

The dude's sister has no specific name.* She is simply an Anglomaniac; though in her, as befits her su-

---

* " Dudine" has been coined since this was written.

perior nature, the malady is not so acute. She wisely refuses to make a martyr of herself to acquire an English waist; and she declines to corrupt her native American speech by a mongrel cockney. She thinks as an American, and talks as an American —though I have heard of her breaking an engagement because her lover called trowsers "pants." Only does she dress as an Englishwoman.

He called trowsers "pants."

And this is really not a bad thing to do. American ladies are tempted by their bright climate into showiness, and a little English corrective, in the shape of sombre colours and less ornamentation, will do good rather than harm. But the styles which English tailors impose on a credulous womankind are often appallingly ugly. Here is a sample taken bodily from an English tailor's advertisement in a New York paper. What curious ideas will Americans have of English girls if this deformity is to be considered a fair sample! Nothing illustrates so well the absurdity of Anglomania in America as the fact that an English tailor should find it profitable to advertise such caricatures. And the prices this audacious

An English girl!

5

Briton demands for his wares! I dare not repeat what
some of my friends tell of his charges: it is almost
incredible. Surely no ridicule can be
too great for such a craze. American
papers are full of it. Perhaps some
good might be done if English papers
took up the cry; for Americans are
sensitive to English criticism. Indeed
it is the only criticism to which they
are sensitive. For a Frenchman's
ridicule they do not care a red cent, as
they would say; and no other Continental nation sees anything in America
to laugh at.

A Dudine.

It is said that one has to go abroad
to learn all about one's own country.
In America I learnt many things
about England of which I had previously no knowledge.
One discovery was that the Prince of Wales introduces
all changes in dress, manners and social arrangements.
I suppose he has as much to do with such changes as
anybody; but I conformed for many years to dicta without knowing who gave the orders. It was from a publication of Harpers' that I first learned to whom I am
indebted for lengthening the lappels
of my coat and giving a curve to the
rim of my hat. I am duly grateful—
nay, more, for I had often declaimed
at fashion when the tailor assured me
that my new coat must differ from the
old one, though the latter satisfied me
in every particular. The paragraph in
Harpers' which revealed my obligations to royalty ends

with a thought worth quoting: "It was said that the dropping of a pebble in the ocean produced a movement which was continued to the utmost confines of the sea. The whim or the comfort of one exalted or dandiacal personage may likewise, in the cut of a coat or the form of a shoe, go round the world. Unconsciously even we republicans are subjects of a king, and the severe and scornful defier of the authority of the British crown defies it in a coat whose 'cut' is a docile acknowledgment of that crown's resistless power. The influence of a social leader is shown in nothing so strongly as in his ability to make two continents wear clothes cut as he chooses."

The picture of the defiant republican declaiming against royalty in a coat fashioned by a king is good. I am glad I saved the extract.

A paper that delights to make fun of that part of the British constitution which is most conspicuous to a republican is the *New Orleans Picayune.* A tirade against Anglomania in that paper, which is now before me, ends with the terse comment: "A troublesome corn on a royal toe of England will change the gait of every society idiot in New York!" This is Carlylean—but not truthful.

There is another type of Anglomaniac. He is not a dude or fashionable exquisite. He is simply a good-hearted, generous fellow, anxious to be hospitable and friendly to a people whose ancestors were also his own. It is hard that such a man should be dubbed a maniac, but it is the truth. The madness, however, lies not so much in the hospitality which he displays as in the worthless character of the guest upon whom it is lavished. I should deplore saying anything that could make the relations of Englishmen and Americans less friendly; but I do not think these relations are any the more cordial because the good-natured Anglomaniac takes up and entertains with lavish hospitality every lordling and snob who visits the Republic. It would be all right if the titled idiot had the heart and head to reciprocate the attention when his American entertainer visits England. But on such occasions we have an exhibition of snobbishness greater than anything Thackeray described. The following is an American's protest against this form of inhospitality. I think it may be read with interest and even profit by certain sections of our fashionable society:

INTERNATIONAL COURTESIES.

The incident of the blackballing of sundry inoffensive and eligible Americans, as Americans, at a London club stimulates reflections which even Mr. Henry James has not exhausted upon the international aspects of " society."

The complications of which the shutting of the doors of the Bachelors' Club against these New Yorkers is the latest, are such as inevitably arise in the intercourse of a strictly classified people like the British with an unclassified people like ourselves. A Briton's social status is very largely fixed by external conditions with which his personal character has little to do. A man of genius may be patronized by members of the class above his own, but if he be also a self-respecting person the patronage will be too obvious to be agreeable. He is admitted on sufferance, and not on the same footing with the persons who belong to " society." The anxiety to appear to be one step higher in the social scale than one really is is the essence of snobbishness, and the snob is distinctly indigenous to Great Britain, being the product of the social environment there prevailing. As a rule an Englishman accepts that station in life, as the English catechism puts it, in which he has been placed, and makes up for the necessity of truckling more or less to people stationed above him in the privilege of bullying

more or less the people stationed below him. An English " swell "
looks upon Americans as Mr. Matthew Arnold did before he came
here. To him they are so many members of the English middle
class. Mr. Arnold's presumption did not survive his visit, but the
English swell is a much thicker-headed person. As Mr. Arnold
himself has said, he is inaccessible to ideas, and his notion that the
United States are populated by degenerate English tradesmen is
ineradicable. He lives with Americans when he is in America, seeing that there is nobody else to live with, but he has not the slight-
est idea of living with them when he is at home. What they resent as snubbing, when he ignores instead of reciprocating their
hospitalities, is to him merely a necessary measure of self-protec-
tion. If a New Yorker should be hospitably treated by guides
and trappers in the Northwest he would feel decently grateful to
them, no doubt, and if he revisited their country he would be at
pains to look them up and receive some more attention from them.
But if the trappers and the guides should come to New York and
expect to be asked to dinner he would be apt to resent their intru-
sion as an impertinence. This is very much the unfeigned feeling
of the British swell toward his American entertainers, and it is
the feeling which the British snob pretends to feel in order to pro-
mote the illusion that he, too, is a swell.

Americans who extend courtesies to Britons who have handles
to their names or who are nearly allied to Britons so equipped are
much deluded if they imagine that these courtesies are received
as courtesies between equals, to be repaid in kind when occasion
offers. A visit to London has wrought a disillusion in the minds
of many of them. It is unfortunately true that many specimens
of the rising generation of the British nobility are as thorough-
going blackguards as incumber the earth, and some of the most
unsavory among them have visited this country. Of course, who-
ever countenances a notorious blackguard by entertaining him
because the blackguard has a title is a snob, and when he is
snubbed and blackballed by the blackguard and the blackguard's
friends a righteous retribution has overtaken him. Not infre
quently the travelling Briton does not wait to reach home before
showing himself ungrateful to his American hosts, but abuses hospitality even when he is in the act of soliciting or of absorbing it.
Such was the case with the Briton whose impudence caused not

only his American entertainers, but his respectable English fellow-travellers, to stand aghast upon a memorable excursion two years ago.

But, then, it is not just to call an English swell a blackguard, nor even to accuse him of being in a general way an ingrate, because he declines to associate on equal terms at home with the persons with whom he was compelled to associate when he was abroad. He may sincerely consider that these people are not his social equals, though he condescended to their society when there was no other to be got. The frankness with which he makes this belief manifest is peculiar to him. But this is connected with one of his most respectable qualities, and that is his indifference to what other people think of him so long as he thinks well of himself. His bump of approbativeness is very small. "What I admire about your Lord Hartington," a foreigner in England is reported in a late book as saying, "is his youbedamnedness." If any American wishes to fathom the depths of the youbedamnedness of the British swell, he need only show social attentions in New York to British peers, and afterward visit London in an innocent expectation that these attentions will be returned.

CHAPTER VI.

A COMMENTARY ON THE GOSPEL OF RELAXATION.

"There is pleasure sure
In being mad, which only madmen
know."—DRYDEN.

F Mulhall is to be trusted as a statistician, there are more insane people in the United States in proportion to population than in any other country except Ireland. The ratio per thousand inhabitants in Europe is 1·6; in the United States it is 3·3. Looking back,we find that this remarkable figure is the product of late years. In 1850 the ratio was only 1·36; in 1860 it was 1·39; in 1870, 1·61; and in 1880 it reached the alarming figure 3·30.

By contrasting the conditions of life in America with those of countries where the insanity rate is low, we have *prima-facie* evidence that the American high rate is due to commercial competition and high-pressure living generally. In Spain and Portugal, for example, where the people are a happy-go-lucky race, and care little for industrial success, the rate is 0·7. In Switzerland, where the people live simple lives, free from business worry, the rate is 1·1.   Similarly in Austria and Russia, the insane rate is low; for though militancy there is a cause of much suffering, the people are free from the contention of an active business life.   In Great Britain, however, where the conditions of life are nearest allied to those in America, the insanity rate is very high, though not so high as in Ireland, where emigration of the healthiest men and women leave the defective to swell the returns in undue proportions.   In Canada the people have less "go" in them than in the States; and there the insane rate is little more than half that of the Republic.

The ratio of increase in America is sufficiently startling; but when we look at the bare figures the contrast is appalling.   Observe the difference between 1850 and 1880:

Year.	Total Insane.	Per 1000 Inhabitants.
1850	31,400	1·36
1860	42,970	1·39
1870	61,960	1·61
1880	168,880	3·3

Of course this tremendous increase has not taken place without remark; but with the fatuity with which men habitually obscure the cause of a disaster, they are explaining the increased madness by saying it is due to the wind!   In the cities around the lakes the favourite theory is that the moist winds from the great freshwater seas are causing the trouble; but if this were so, Canada's insanity rate should be even higher than that of the Republic, since a greater proportion of its population lives on the lakes.   The explanation is suggestive of the German schoolboy's song,

> "Du bist verrückt, mein Kind;
> Du hast ein Kopf voll Wind!"

The fierce struggle for existence in America is shown not only by crowded madhouses. It is conspicuous in the wild rush of the city streets, and in the careworn faces of men. Herbert Spencer told the Americans, when he preached to them his gospel of relaxation, that persistent activity had with them reached an extreme from which there must begin a counterchange — a reaction. "Everywhere," said he, "I have been struck with the number of faces

English methods.

which told in strong lines of the burdens that had to be borne. I have been struck, too, with the large proportion of gray-haired men; and inquiries have brought out the fact that with you the hair commonly begins to turn some ten years earlier than with us." I have several acquaintances in America whose hair was tinged with gray before they were thirty years of age. Everywhere one meets men who have suffered from nervous collapse, or hears of men killed by overwork—"died in harness," as they say in America. Even children in schools display "the same feverishness and absence of repose," to borrow the expression of the Rev. Mr. Fraser who reported on American educational systems to our government a few years ago.

And what is the good of all this strife? Well may the astonished stranger ask, when puzzled natives thus speak:

"The United States is a paradox: forty-three billions of wealth; yet work is hard to get, and leisure scarcely exists. The nation grows richer, but the individual works harder. The problem of living gets more complicated, instead of getting simpler. Mr. Atkinson tells us that we have saved fifteen billions of dollars since 1860. Where are they? Have they earned us any leisure? Have they quieted our anxious business worries? 'Ten men can now feed one thousand, one man shoe a thousand;' why do not the nine hundred and ninety-nine have time for rest and culture? 'We produce enough in six months to last for a year'; why have we not six months every year for education and enjoyment? 'We make two billions now for every billion made twenty years ago;' why do we still have but $119 apiece a year to live upon? It is not our wealth that needs to be explained, but our poverty."*

The evil consequences of this absorption are further seen in the stunted forms and pale faces of the children of nervous men. They are seen in the solitary lives of the women. In summer women crowd the mountain hotels and seaside resorts; their husbands visit them from Saturday till Monday, and hammer away at business during the week. They are seen in the success of political jobbers—low foreigners who find the misgovernment of a city or a State more remunerative than carrying mortar and bricks up a ladder. The best men of America are absorbed in the struggle for wealth;

---

* Herbert Putnam in *Citizen*, Aug. 1886.

the government of the city and State is left to bar-room politicians and peculating officials. Here it is that the gross selfishness of the American business man is seen at its worst. He is aware of all the corruption and dishonesty that pollute the City Hall or the State legislature. He occasionally swears a great oath when a piece of jobbery of unusual magnitude and audacity becomes known; but he goes on making his personal pile bigger and bigger, committing the government to Sheol and the Irish.

Examples of official incompetency and worse can be gathered from every newspaper; yet such is the public indifference that in every city there are thousands of citizens who do not take the trouble to be registered and to vote. And of those who do vote, the majority is so completely controlled by one or other of the party machines, that the real voice of the people—the Vox Dei —is completely stifled in the ballot-box. Occasionally the citizens rise up in anger and abolish the corrupt administration. Then they settle down again to acquiring each other's property, and soon another "ring" is gilding itself with taxpayers' dollars.

The man who thus sacrifices wife, children, city and State to his desire to "get on" does not escape the searing of the finer feelings inseparable from prolonged selfishness. Add to this the effect of forty years' industrial campaigning, with little relaxation and no cultivation except that found in morning newspapers and daily price-lists, and we get an ideal "successful business man:"

> "Through life's dark road his sordid way he wends,
> An incarnation of fat dividends."

The superabundant energy of Americans, which so often takes the form of commercial wrestling, is sometimes attributed to their bright invigorating climate. And that there is some truth in the explanation is obvious to all who have had opportunities of contrasting the listless condition of mind and body engendered by a damp, muggy day in England, with the exhilarating glow excited by the crisp atmosphere of an American winter's day, when the heart beats a joyous tune to which every fibre responds in unison. In California one constantly experiences this delightful buoyancy of mind and body; and many a gigantic bubble-scheme has been floated into its rare atmosphere, which has hopelessly collapsed as soon as it passed into the denser air of other regions. In Denver, at some seasons, solid-looking business men trip along the streets with a lightness that is almost sylph-like; and frequently in New York one feels like Tommy Upmore, when his expanding joyousness carried him over the tree-tops like a balloon. But though climate may account for much of the overflowing energy of Americans, it does not account for the limitation of effort to personal ends. The fact is that work has become a kind of war; and the average Yankee values an industrial victory as highly as the red-skinned American prized his enemy's scalp-lock. They are both successful competitors; and there is not much difference in the character of their rewards.

The spirit of competition pervades every detail of the American's life. Not only is his business-life ruled by it: it gives form to such amusements as he allows himself. If he owns horses, they must be able to trot as fast as those of his business rival, and to that end his buggy or sleigh is made as light as possible. Everywhere boxing-matches are well attended; and pugilists sometimes receive homage rarely accorded to more worthy men.

Bliss—long drawn out.

Here is a description of the home-coming of a Philadelphia pugilist, after an encounter with the Boston champion:

" Cleopatra herself when she went sailing up the Cydnus to meet Antony hardly travelled in more state than did Mr. McCaffrey in his journey from the Broad Street station to his Eighth Street saloon. If his name instead of being Dominick had been Horatius, and if instead of fighting a fellow-creature for money he had been saving Rome by keeping a bridge over the Tiber, he could hardly have been decorated with more signal marks of admiration. A cheering crowd met him when the train stopped; triumphant music announced his presence; a band of enthusiastic friends, while the strains of ' Hail to the Chief ' floated away on the Pennsylvania air, lifted him bodily from his feet and bore him aloft on their shoulders to a splendid carriage drawn by four prancing horses; a body-guard of eight hundred devoted fellow-citizens followed the carriage down Chestnut Street; directly in front of the imposing chariot ran a goodly number of the youth of the city, making constant proclamation as they ran that the Chief was coming; at Eleventh and Chestnut streets three fair Philadelphia maidens—of course intended to typify Faith, Hope and Charity, although none of the local papers say so—waved their handkerchiefs at the Chief, who in turn ' bowed modestly.'

Thus came the pugilist home. So Philadelphia welcomed the return of Dominick McCaffrey. John Welsh had no such a re-

 ception on his return from Europe. But then he had only been Minister at the Court of St. James. Benjamin H. Brewster had no such reception on his return from Washington. But then he had only been Attorney-General of the United States. Daniel Dougherty had no such a reception on his return from his most successful lecturing tour. But then he is only a great orator. Dominick McCaffrey is a pugilist. The rising generation in Philadelphia can draw its own moral."

It need hardly be said that "the rising generation of Philadelphia" here meant is that portion of it which makes the most noise and does the city the least credit. Corresponding crowds would greet with enthusiasm a native pugilist in any city; but to admit this would have spoilt the laugh which this New York journalist wished to raise at the expense of the Quaker City.

Athletic clubs are common enough in American cities; but the competitive instinct crops out even in these. Professional walking- and skating-matches sometimes partake of the nature of a horrible torturing, so prolonged and keen is the struggle. Here is a description of a victim of a six days' walking-match:

"Fitzgerald's face—unshaven, uncouth, distorted and ungainly, withered by the tremendous strain and lined like a cobweb— was a more repulsive sight during the last three days of the match than anything in the Eden Musée. His eyes were sluggish, bloodshot and heavy, and encompassed by huge purple circles. His cheeks had so sunk in that the contour of the teeth could almost have been seen through them, and every move-  ment was an illustration of acute agony. He swung his arms painfully, his head dropped on his chest, his shoulder-blades stuck out sharply from his attenuated body, his legs dragged lamely one after the other, and the muscles of his neck twitched nervously at every step. He dragged himself steadfastly ahead, never turning his eyes to the right or left, until he came to the scorer's stand, when he painfully and laboriously turned his face toward the figures to see that they were correctly given."

Others are described as even more pitiable. The analytic journalist adds:

"Night after night and day after day thousands of people poured into the garden and hung for hours over the rail staring at the faces of the poor wretches who were dragging themselves around the track. There seemed to be a sort of morbid fascination in it for the crowd. A man would get a position along the rail where he could see the walkers for an instant as they passed on their rounds. Here he would stand for five or six hours in the stifling atmosphere, pushed and jostled by the crowd, just for the chance of catching a glimpse of the faces of the toiling pedestrians as they came around the track. Everybody who came in exclaimed at the revolting appearance of the men, and then crowded eagerly for a place where they could catch a closer view of them."

There is surely not much difference between our nineteenth-century humanity and that humanity of Roman days which found its most inspiring diversion in watching men and beasts fight to the death. The amusements of a people are always in harmony with its conditions. The conditions of the old Romans called for great personal courage, prompt decision in danger, unswerving devotion to the state, and even cruelty. In the amphitheatre these qualities were exhibited in their highest degree. In America in modern days, the qualities most admired are those which have made it the most industrial of nations; and exhibitions of energy, perseverance, endurance, and that indefinable mixture of them all, "grit," will continue

in favour as long as the present conception of success prevails.   A couple of years ago a man skated on roller-
skates 1055 miles in six days, and died a few weeks later
from exhaustion—it was called by another name by his
friends.   The tortures which this wretched creature
and his competitors underwent were described in ghastly
detail by the principal New York papers.   The horrible
looks of the men, the pressing forward of the crowd—
every revolting circumstance was printed in newspapers
which in America hold the position of the *Times, Standard* or *Daily News* in England.

Every amusement which allows betting is in favour in
America.   Baseball- and trotting-matches, horse-races,
boxing-matches, iceboat-races and yachting are favourite sports.   Betting on the exchange is not an amuse-

ment in America
any more than it is
elsewhere.   It is a
grave   soul-killing
business, as repug-
nant to every fine
sentiment of human-
ity as slaughtering cattle.   That it should prevail to the
extent it does in America implies a depth of commercial
degradation discouraging to those who are ever looking
for signs of progress in the race.   This aspect of American life is as repulsive as its walking- and skating-
matches.

Perhaps nothing so well illustrates the difference between the English and American character as the national games of cricket and baseball.   The British game
is slow and irksome to an American.   The deliberation
with which the "overs" are made is insupportable to

one of his quick, time-sparing habits; while the long-drawn contest, often lasting a couple of days, is simply impossible in a country where time is so valuable that love-letters are said to be written on the type-writer. The finest game of baseball—which is the lineal descendant, improved by careful breeding, of the children's game of "rounders"—is completed within two hours; and every emotion from exultation to despair may be crowded into that short time. Baseball is short and exciting; cricket long and often monotonous, like the performance in a Chinese theatre.

That sparrows fight is a fact known to every people among whom this domestic little pet makes its home. A philanthropist introduced a number of English sparrows into America, and the people welcomed them with the heartiness they extend to everything English. Houses were placed in trees and on telegraph-poles for the accommodation of the little Britons, who prospered and multiplied at a rate which put the German immigrant to shame. Before the sparrows came, it was impossible to walk with comfort under the trees which in American towns are planted along the streets: ugly worms and caterpillars dropped down, and crawled over woman's bonnets and down men's collars. The sparrows ate up the worms, and thus fulfilled the task expected of them. Then the great American nation discovered that the sparrow was a nuisance. It fought everything that could fight, and drove away the things that could not fight. With shocking lack of filial respect, it hesitated not to fight its own father and mother, and attacked its cousins, and its sisters and its aunts. In brief, it was a demoralizing influence; and a wail went up from the press of the land. But the sparrows had

6

settled down for life, as is the habit of English colonists. It is this simple trait that makes English colonies permanent and successful. The Frenchman goes abroad to make money which he intends to spend in Paris. The Briton settles down and makes his home in the new country to which he goes, and henceforth regards England only as his headquarters. If the American philanthropist wanted colonists of itinerant habits he should have introduced French sparrows. To introduce Britons was a grave oversight of first principles—a mistake possible only to a philanthropist, with his love of direct remedies.

The pugnacity of the now-acclimated sparrow has been turned to good account by the American Chinee. He has made it a means of relaxation from the wash-tub and ironing-board. He has trained the sparrow to fight scientifically. A Philadelphia reporter who saw such a prize-fight says:

"The sparrows' wings were cut and their tails were cropped close. Their bills were almost white where they had been sandpapered to make their little beaks as sharp as a needle's point. One of the sparrows  had a little piece of red ribbon wrapped around its leg to distinguish it from the other. Hop Chung Lung, who is one of the silent partners of the gambling house, then sized up the birds with a sporting man's eye, and offered to bet ten 'plunks' (dollars) that the bird with the red ribbon on its right leg would kill the other. There were no takers until Bun Sun Low had dropped the birds in the pit. The moment this was done the sparrow that had no ribbon on it plunged at the other and pecked a mouthful of feathers out of its head. This caused a chuckle all around, and Charlie Lee, the Tenth Street laundryman, covered Hop Chung

Lung's ten ' plunks.' This added fresh excitement to the fight. The bird with the red leg was the gamest, and made a lunge at his antagonist. In another moment he pecked the other bird in the throat, and his needle-pointed bill did deadly work. The one-eyed bird toppled over and fell on the sand dead. Other fights followed, and when the fourth brace had fought for three or four minutes Chung Wat told Bun Sun Low to stop the fight, and the spectators were told the sport was over."

There are two sections of the American people to whom the preaching the Gospel of Relaxation is a work of supererogation: the western farmers and the coloured people. The ambitions of both classes are narrowly circumscribed. That of the western farmer is well indicated in the following catechism:

Q. What is the American farmer's ambition?

A. To buy more land.

Q. What does he want more land for?

A. To grow more corn.

Q. Why does he want more corn?

A. To raise more hogs.

Q. Why does he want more hogs?

A. To sell, in order to buy more land, to grow more corn, to raise more hogs, to sell in order to buy more land.

And so in monotonous round the western farmer's ambition passes from land to corn, and hogs, and land. There is nothing wearing in this; and the farmer lives a quiet happy life which is unknown to dwellers in cities, with their ceaseless strivings, disappointments and heart-burnings.

The coloured people are a happy contented race. Wherever they are one hears their merry chatter and the loud yah-yah of their laugh. With song and jest they kill time and dull care, as they lounge in groups on southern wharves and levees, or sit idly swinging their feet on the edge of a railway platform. Carlyle gives a funny picture of the negro who eats the inside of a pumpkin, puts half the empty rind on his head, sits in the other half, and then blinks at the world in satisfied comfort. Carlyle was angry at the picture. He wanted this ruminating animal to come out of his pumpkin, and work. "Every man has a right to be forced to work," scolded the philosopher, with his usual contempt for logic. But then he had scolded the workers; and when told that Americans double their numbers every twenty-five years, doubted if to have forty million dollar-hunters in the world were any better than to have twenty million dollar-hunters. Poor old man! He hunted too

—and lived long enough to see the futility of his own particular chase. For my part, the picturesque darky in his pumpkin is a more agreeable sight than the same darky perspiring in the noonday sun, exercising his "right to be forced to work."

Most of the personal service is in the hands of coloured people. The hotels are everywhere full of them; and they make cheerful, ready servants in a house. They are very musical. A score of coloured waiters at a summer - hotel often contain enough talent to form a glee club; and during the warm evenings their plaintive songs, still tinged with the melancholy of slavery, awake the echoes of the woods, and thrill the listener with that luxurious sadness which so often characterizes the music of a conquered race—like the minor music of the Irish peasantry. The prettiest song that ever originated in America—"'Way down upon the Suwanee River"—is of this character—in which are interwoven "*les pleurs du peuple et les fleurs du printemps.*" With a skiff moored in some quiet creek, the darky fisherman symbolizes his race: perhaps asleep, but always happy and comfortable, caring little about the scaly tribe until forced to care by hunger. An infusion of negro contentment into the Yankee character would do Uncle Sam good. His energy and enterprise and industry require to be tempered by that quality which the French call *insouciance.*

CHAPTER VII.

SOCIAL ATAVISM; OR OLD THINGS UNDER A NEW NAME.

"To tear down the sky in order to catch larks is wasteful extravagance, and should be forbidden by law."—*A New Laputa.*

T is well known to breeders of pigeons, rabbits and dogs that the offspring of pure-blooded parents often shows a low-breed taint. The litter of a high-bred lop-eared rabbit often contains an animal possessing the appearance and character of a remote wild progenitor. The new-born ass sometimes shows the zebra-markings of a distant ancestor, and horses are sometimes born with three toes. In plants, too, the same tendency is observed: peaches sometimes appear on a nectarine-tree. Men and women, too, revert to ancestral types. We all know some one who is the image of his grandfather, and not a bit like his father. And ancestral character, as well as appearance, is apt thus to break out in later generations. Some men, indeed, seem to inherit with great directness the instincts and desires of some ancestor who lived among the cave men in a paleolithic age, while others, with some traits adapted to nineteenth-century civilization, are ever ready to drop into the habits and feelings of that hairy ancestor who lived in tree-tops, ages before the cave men.

This reversion to ancestral types Mr. Darwin called atavism.

Societies as well as individuals sometimes display a retrograde tendency. Laws and customs which they have outgrown, and which are no longer fitted to their advanced condition, grow up afresh, just as the canine teeth of men occasionally acquire the prominence of fangs. In America the highest social development the world has ever seen is accompanied by the most conspicuous examples of social atavism.

And let me here explain what I mean by the highest social development. I do not claim for America the highest development of literature, music, or the fine arts. Such a claim would be absurd. Neither do I claim for it the greatest diversity of social elements; for I believe the differentiation of parts has proceeded to a greater extent in England or even France than in America. The highest social development here meant is that implied by the term " industrial," which has been so often used to characterize the Republic.

The lowest forms of society are those simple communities in which all men are equal; just as the lowest forms of animal life are those of which the parts are alike. A chicken with its great diversity of parts— bone, muscle, nerve, claws and horny beak—is more highly evolved than the egg, with its simple division into yolk and white. So is it with societies. Progress begins when men cease to be equal—when the best, bravest, or most cunning become leaders. It continues as these leaders acquire power to coerce the other members into united action. And when at last we reach a point at which men have lost all individuality and have become merely parts of a complex machine, directed by one mind, we get a perfect example of the militant society. Germany and Russia are the nearest of modern societies to this type. To see that such a condition is essential to the existence of the society at some stages of its growth, we have only to imagine what would happen to Germany if the condition in which Tacitus found it could be suddenly renewed. The great empire would be split into multitudinous fragments, none larger than an American township. These fragments, corresponding to the old tribal divisions, would be further subdivided into clans, and these again into families; and the members of the families, owning but partial allegiance to the patriarchal head, would act as their idiosyncrasies prompted them. It is absurd to ask if such a Germany could withstand for a moment the onslaught of a united France. Forty-six million Germans with forty-six million notions as to the relative merits of the chassepot or mitrailleuse, would be wiped out of existence while discussing means of defence. But forty-six million Germans with only one opinion, can certainly defend themselves successfully against thirty-eight million Frenchmen with opinions as numerous and varied as their political parties. This greater unity of mind and purpose is a factor which will tell in favour of the Fatherland in the next war.

But this type of society is not a final one. When a nation has acquired the right to live unmolested, its progress begins to take a new course. The individual gradually regains his individuality; for now his person and property are less frequently taken for the defence of the State. The society now advances from militancy towards industrialism; from socialism to individualism. England is advancing along this line; and owing to her immunity from invasion, she is in the van of European progress. America is the only nation which has reached a stage in which industrialism predominates over militancy. England annually spends about sixty-three millions sterling on war, and debts incurred by war, while her civil charges are less than twenty millions. America spends but ten millions on war preparations; while her civil and pension lists amount to over seventy millions. Her police army of twenty-five thousand men is scarcely to be reckoned a sign of militancy. And this is what is meant by assigning to America the first place among nations.

The absence of rank is another sign of America's superiority. A concomitant of declining militancy is the transfer of power from the ruler to the people; and if this process goes far, the ruler falls into the ranks again, and equality results. An illustration is at hand. The Czar of Russia lately killed an officer who put his hand to his breast as if to draw a revolver. Under a military *régime* there is no tribunal to judge and punish this man who kills another in misapprehension of his purpose. But under an industrial *régime* the President of the United States or the Prince of Wales would be tried even for assault, and punished equally with any other citizen if found guilty.

With decreasing demands upon the individual come decreased restraints upon his actions. No longer required to repel invaders, he is at liberty to move about at will, to make contracts with other men, to engage in manufactures, to buy and to sell; and under the perfect industrial *régime*, he is subject to no restrictions except those imposed by the equal freedom of others. And thus is reached the political ideal of equal rights.

If such an industrial community suddenly begins to make elaborate preparation for war, it reverts to an ancestral form. If it establishes ranks, or grades of men, its return to a less perfect type is none the less marked. If it deprives individuals of that liberty of action which is limited only by the equal rights of all, its atavism is again conspicuous. The reader will now see what is meant when it is said that in America the highest social development the world has ever seen, is accompanied by the most marked examples of social atavism.

And now let us look at these examples—political, social and personal.

When English writers on political economy wish to illustrate in the clearest way the mischievous effects of governmental interference with commerce, they go back several centuries to quote the usury laws. In every part of America the usury laws are operative just as they were in Moses' time or in the time of the Stuarts. And can their absurdity be better marked than by the fact that different States have different rates of legal interest, ranging from five to ten per cent?

Congress recently undertook to regulate commerce between States. It was thought by sapient legislators that managers of railways and steamboat companies did not know their business; so they passed the Interstate Commerce Bill, which among other things fixed the charges of railway companies and other carriers. The act has operated mischievously in numerous unforeseen ways. It is oppressive to theatrical companies; it is ruining some branches of trade with Canada; it has crippled many forms of business, and produced com plications of the most unexpected character. Many of its clauses cannot be enforced. and it is a complete vindication of the saying that restrictions will not "stay put." The prophet runs little risk of being discredited when he predicts that this meddling piece of legislation will have to be annulled.

In April, 1887, over one hundred persons were arrested in New York for Sunday trading. Policemen in plain clothes went about the city, tempting people to break the old Sabbatarian laws which had almost become a dead letter. Some persons were arrested for shaving policemen; some for selling them liquor; some for selling them such essentials to Sabbath cleanliness and comfort as a handkerchief; and  one poor old woman was locked up for being persuaded to sell a lamp-shade! For be it known that in the Republic a disguised policeman may incite to wrong, and then arrest the wrong-doer without the formality of a warrant! And by a curious course of reasoning, the one who incites to the wrong, and in its commission acts as accomplice, is rewarded rather than punished! This method of assisting crime, by treachery, deceit and other detestable means, is the way in which the law tries to keep the Sabbath day holy!

In several States men are prohibited from buying alcoholic beverages at any time. A man who wants brandy, say for his sick wife, must go to a magistrate, and swear an affidavit that he does not intend to drink it himself, before he is permitted to buy a stated small quantity at the druggist's. This is to train men to self-control and temperance!

A spirited foreign policy moulded after that of

Beaconsfield, is a clear case of retrogression in the peaceful industrial republic; but the United States has its Jingo party, headed by a candidate for the Presidency. If this enterprising leader should ever be elected, we shall have our list of examples of atavism greatly prolonged.

In the county of Columbia, Pennsylvania, a young man recently brought an action against his mother to recover damages for the loss of a dog, which he claimed she bewitched, so that it ran in a circle until it died of exhaustion. Shades of Cotton Mather and Judge Jeffries, are ye not happy again! The trial showed that there is an almost general belief in witchcraft, charms and magic spells among the farm population in these localities, and that there are many old women who are regularly consulted by young and old, and in whose arts and supernatural powers they put faith.

About a year ago, at Mount Morris, Michigan, a whole family of sixteen persons went crazy over the belief that their premises were bewitched, and began cutting nicks in the ears of their pigs and cows to let the devil out. In Danbury, Connecticut, at the same time they were curing long-standing rheumatism by the charms of black snakes.

Every day, advertisements worded as below appear in newspapers throughout America. These are from a single day's issue of the *New York World:*

" At her parlors, 63 4th ave., between 9th and 10th sts., Mrs. Dr. Hill can be consulted on all affairs of life, being a celebrated business clairvoyant, astrologist and palmist, who has a reputation throughout the world for her accurate and truthful readings of the past, present and future; removes evil influences and family estrangements; unites the separated and causes speedy marriage; brings success to the unsuccessful, and tells when to make profitable investments; consultations $1; also tells full name and shows picture of the one you will marry, for $1; strangers from other cities will save time and disappointment by calling on this genuine clairvoyant before going elsewhere; life reading and picture by mail on receipt of $1; lock of hair, full name and date of birth."

"Arrived from Europe.—Mme. De Varney,the world renowned, highly celebrated clairvoyant; seventh daughter; born with veil and second sight; while in a trance will truthfully reveal every hidden mystery in life; removes troubles, evil influences; settles lovers' quarrels, brings separated together, causes speedy and happy marriages, and tells if the one you love is true or false; advice given to gentlemen on business, and to young men what is best adapted for speedy riches; if you have been disappointed by others, judge not all alike. All in search of truth and satisfaction, call at 413 6th ave.; calls received Sundays."

"Mme. Zingara, gypsy, 289 6th ave., cor. 18th st. It is well known throughout the world that gypsies are only reliable; removes evil influences, causes love, marriages; advises in business, law, contracts, wills, divorces, absent friends, health; lucky charms free; seen on Sunday."

"Zibola, clairvoyant, will read your destiny, good or bad; withholds nothing; if in trouble, call at once; seen Sunday, 229 8th ave., near 22d st.; fee, 50c."

"Attention!—Consultation on business, lawsuits, absent friends, deaths, separations, date of marriage, everything revealed; no equal; fee moderate; satisfaction or no pay. Mrs. Pierce, celebrated clairvoyant, 457 3d ave., near 31st st."

"Mme. Bennett, celebrated clairvoyant and palmist, consults on all matters. 74 3d ave., near 11th st., one flight; hours, 9 to 9."

"Mrs. Arnold, reliable trance medium; satisfaction guaranteed. 137 West 23d st."

"Dr. Laroche, French trance clairvoyant, asking no questions, gives the names of his sitters, ladies their married and maiden names; reunites the loved who are separated; tells whom and when you are to marry; advises in business, law, contracts, wills, divorces, absent friends, health, etc. ; 9 to 9. 177 3d ave., above 16th."

"Edith, colored clairvoyant; great secret discovered; private advice given. 216 West 28th st."

"Lady Stanley, only true, gifted, most wonderful English palmist, reveals past and future; satisfaction, no pay. 366 3d ave., near 27th st."

Her ladyship must find the Republic a palmy place after England, where she and her craft must hide in holes and corners with the constant fear of arrest. For at home the Government kindly protects us from witches and wizards, as it used to protect us from Quakers.

At the time of writing I am constantly hearing of a man in New York who is telling fortunes by palmistry, and getting scores of otherwise intelligent people to cross his hand with a ten-dollar bill. But here I ought to be silent; for this clever personage, who is being received into good society, is an Englishman. And is there not an English guide-book to palmistry "dedicated by permission to Her Serene Highness Princess Victoria Mary of Teck"! O land of anomalies!

The whipping-post survives in the south, and is about to be revived in Pennsylvania. Though England has not abolished this remnant of the mediæval torture-chamber, the retrogression is none the less marked in Pennsylvania—the Quaker State. Centuries of judicial torture have not taught us that men cannot be whipped into a high morality. The rod which produces vengeful feelings and a surly temper in the schoolboy is not more soothing when laid across the back of a man. Judicial methods will have to be very much reformed when men better understand men's natures.

Here is a suggestive newspaper item concerning this mode of torture:

"WILMINGTON, DEL., Nov. 21, 1885.—A large crowd, including seven amateur photographers with cameras, attended the whipping at New Castle to-day. William Turner (colored), for larceny of a watch, took five lashes; Alexander R. Fields, charged with larceny, ten lashes; and John Manlove and William H. Morris, colored burglars, stood an hour in the pillory and received twenty lashes each."

It reminds one of the Parisian photographers who, with the most improved instantaneous arrangements, were present at the public execution by shooting of the bishops, and the communists. The ages clasp hands! Civilization reaches across the gulf of time, and receives a sympathetic handshake from the grizzly spectre of barbarism. We can imagine with what satisfaction these amateur photographers would have exposed a plate on Attila's pyramid of skulls, or the burning of Latimer, or Nero's living torches; and we are justified in supposing that if they felt any sorrow at all, it would only be because the flames were not actinic. These are the men who can leap across the dead centuries into an earlier age: who display the zebra-markings of remote ancestors!

In a land that claims to be the freest in the world, it seems an anomaly that you may not cross the road at some parts of Central Park. You are " positively " forbidden to do so, lest you be knocked down by a passing vehicle; and if you persist you will probably be taken to jail by a policeman whose powers of arrest are limited only by his physical strength. This is nearly as funny as a cricket-match in France I once heard of: a gendarme stood by the bowler, and cautioned him not to send swift balls, because they would hurt the batter if they struck him! And I have heard some timid people plead that football ought to be forbidden by law, as a dangerous game. It would hardly be more absurd to demand that shin-pads be provided for the players by government and paid for out of the taxes.

This prohibition from crossing a carriage track, is curiously incongruous in a country where locomotives dash through towns and over level crossings with little or no warning. Writing of this, Mr. Archibald Forbes says: "The American theory, bluntly put, is that since it may be presumed a man has a greater interest in keeping alive than any one else has in his doing so, the onus of self-preservation primarily rests on himself. The Australian theory, on the other hand, is that it is the duty of the State by every possible precaution and enactment to take care that the citizen be protected from his own carelessness. As in England so in Australia, every railroad is fenced, and every level crossing protected assiduously by gates." Here is a strange confusion of ideas! Mr. Forbes has completely inverted the positions. A person has either a right to pass along a public street or he has not. [The proposition seems absurd—out of America.] If he has, he ought to be allowed to do so without the danger of being knocked down and killed by a locomotive. If he has not, he should be excluded from the street. Surely no reasonable being will contend that the English and Australian methods are not better than those of America. In American towns you sometimes hear a bell, a sudden rush, and before you know what is the matter, a train dashes through the street you are about to cross. And how about level crossings ? Here is no question of "his own carelessness." No care will prevent accidents. Horses will take fright, people will stumble, or be hard of hearing, or blind. That some Americans do not live up to what Mr. Forbes calls the American theory is

proved by the frequent protests which find their way
into newspapers.

" During the past year *The World* has chronicled the death of
at least one person a day at railroad crossings in New Jersey. In
consideration for killing this number the railroad companies have
paid a sum wholly inadequate to the loss—probably not over twenty-
five thousand dollars altogether. . . . The effect is apparent. Grade
crossings—an abomination in an age of progress—exist without
number. Gates are few, far between, and generally cumbersome
and rotten. Trains dash across the crowded streets of Newark,
Jersey City, Camden, Elizabeth and New Brunswick with little
if any diminution of speed. Human life is placed at a discount.
These facts are well known. Instances are too numerous to require specification, and yet nothing is done to check this daily
slaughter. This is a cold and unfeeling earth upon which we
live, but there is no reason why the railroads should have the
whole of it."

Indianapolis has been called the City of Concentric
Circles, because of the many railway girdles which sur-
round it. Every approach to the city is cut up with
level crossings. Some friends of mine who live just
outside the city, have to send the children across these
railway tracks to school. When they are safely over,
the children telephone home that they are still alive.
Between a compulsory law requiring attendance at school
and half a dozen railway crossings forbidding it, the
American parent is sometimes in a pitiful dilemma.

In towns the danger is increased by the frequency of
tram-lines, for which a railway track may be easily
mistaken. Indeed they are practically the same, and
are called by the same name—railroads. In many towns
the train goes right through the streets, sometimes—as at
Syracuse—behind a tram-car, and running so near the

7

sidewalks that you might toss a coin into a fruit-shop and receive your purchase through the car window.

A bill was not long since introduced into the Georgia legislature (as a jest, it is said) to impose an annual tax of $2.50 on bachelors. It was considered such an outrage, that the member who introduced it was challenged by an editor to a duel. There are scores of bills introduced into the State legislatures more outrageous than this: so many, indeed, that there would be initiated a state of private war if every foolish bill-maker were challenged to a duel. Even at this late day we find legislators so ignorant of history, as to attempt to fix prices by enactment. The rates for telephones, the price of gas, the dividends of corporations, are thus fixed in New York State. There, too, a compulsory Saturday half-holiday has been legalized; an attempt has been made to erect free Turkish baths supported by taxation; a law has been passed against catching trout less than six inches long, so that you have to take a foot-rule with you when you go a fishing; a bill has been introduced to build grain elevators to be operated by

Legislators drafting
a bill.

the State; and, as if to make the Assembly at Albany seem ludicrous as well as ignorant, a leader of the legislature has just had passed a bill making it a misdemeanor to feed or harbour sparrows! Why don't these sages make it penal to feed and harbour mosquitoes, or to have the small-pox? Well may Puck exclaim, "What fools these mortals be!" They look to the law for protection; but what is to protect them against the law?

It has been frequently noted that men will act collectively in a manner which each, as an individual, would consider foolish or despicable. Not long since I saw the students of Columbia College—a set of well-bred young gentlemen—march, at night, through the streets of New York wearing night-shirts over their clothes. They were celebrating the anniversary of their college. But there was unquestionably not an individual among them who would have walked down Fifth Avenue alone in his night-shirt. When a man makes a fool of himself, he likes to have company. It must be an allied reason that allows so much folly to crystallize into laws.

Many obsolete offences are preserved in America. These, as survivals, are not examples of atavism; but they are of the same nature, and are too interesting not to be mentioned here.

At Washington, Pennsylvania, a man was recently tried and found guilty of barratry. The newspaper report defines this strange offence :

"It seems that the defendant has for years made himself prominent as a mischief-maker, and the practice has become so frequent that the good citizens of the neighborhood deemed it necessary to sit down on him."

Here is another legal curiosity :

EAVESDROPPING.

PHILADELPHIA, July 8.—Assistant District Attorney Kinsey sent into the Grand Jury to-day an indictment in the following words:

"That Louisa Ehrline on the 21st of June, 1886, and on each and every day thence continually until the day of the finding of this indictment, was and is a common eavesdropper, and on each and all of said days and times did listen about the houses and under the windows and eaves of the houses of the citizens then and there dwelling, bearing tattle and repeating the same in the hearing of other persons, to the common nuisance of the citizens of this Commonwealth and against the peace and dignity of the Commonwealth of Pennsylvania."

The grand jury returned a true bill.

Scolds are still amenable to law in Pennsylvania:

" PHILADELPHIA, Oct. 23 [1886] (*Special*).—On the evidence of fifteen people at the Central Station this afternoon Mrs. A. Clauden and Mrs. Kate Lee were held in $600 bail for being common scolds. The testimony showed that the women were fighting all day and half the night, and made the lives of their neighbors miserable."

Actions at law are often instituted to recover damages for alienating a wife's or husband's affections! And I once read of a woman who sought to recover five thousand dollars damages, because her husband, an expert swimmer, was drowned while bathing from the defendant's pavilion!

A short time ago two young girls in Connecticut having been seen at a roller-skating rink in defiance of their mother's orders, and being afraid to return home, took train to New York. The sweetheart of one of them telegraphed to the New York police and had them arrested, and held until he came to take them home. Here is a wondrous power given to an individual. A person may telegraph, in an assumed name if he likes, to some distant town, and cause the arrest of anybody he wishes to annoy! A lunatic with a mania for having people arrested might create some curious complications under this system of primitive officialism. In America arrests seem to be the panacea for every evil. Is a per-

son a gambler and likely to impoverish his family; his
wife has him arrested. Is a lover backward in fulfilling
his promise; his sweetheart has him arrested. Does a
woman suspect her husband of an inten-
tion to elope; she has him arrested. Is a
man rude to a policeman, or does the
policeman think him so; he is arrested.
I have seen in Chicago a driver taken from
his cart and lodged in jail for telling a
policeman to go to Sheol; and in New
York a gentleman was recently arrested
because his horse ran away with him, and
after throwing him, knocked down a road-
mender. And when arrested what be-
comes of all these people ? Well, the
gambler is made to promise to mend his

A moral prophy-
lactic.

ways or make provision for his family; the lover must
show cause for his delay, or else marry the girl, often
on the spot; the suspected husband has to declare his
faithfulness; the man who had the temerity to brave a
policeman is cautioned or "sent up," as seems best
suited to his degree of offence. As a curious bit of
romance and an illustration of grandmotherly republi-
canism, I quote the following from a New York paper.
Similar cases can be found any day.

AUGUST MUST MARRY.

A YOUNG GERMAN DETAINED IN THE TOMBS UNTIL HE AND CHRISTINA ARE MARRIED.

When Christina Swan and August Morio eloped from Hamburg
together three months ago they came to this city with the intention of marrying at once. August took his sweetheart to the home
of his brother, in First street, and not having sufficient money to

enable him to support her he requested that she wait a few weeks. Christina secured a situation as a domestic and August remained at the home of his brother, Henry. The latter being quite poor and August being an experienced carpenter, August managed to assist his brother in maintaining his household and supporting a remarkably pretty wife. The wife recognized August's genius and admired him, while the newly arrived brother fell desperately in love with Henry's wife. He forgot all about his sweetheart, Christina, and she, discovering how matters stood, applied at Castle Garden for assistance in compelling August to keep his promise to her and marry her.

August was arrested on Christina's complaint and lodged in Ludlow Street Jail. Promising to marry her he was released, but he failed to keep his promise, and ridding himself of the girl he induced Henry and his wife to move to No. 37 First street, a few blocks from their former residence. Christina, after vainly endeavoring to find her lover, again applied at Castle Garden, and Detective Groden was detailed to find the recreant lover. Yesterday he arrested August just as he was entering his brother's home in First street, and was taken to the Tombs Court, where he promised to marry Christina to-day.

"I would have married her before," said August, "but my sister-in-law induced me not to do so."

"And he won't marry her now," screamed Henry's wife, who was present. "He loves me, and I won't have him marrying a woman he does not love. He is mine."

"But you are married," interposed Justice White.

"It don't make any difference," screamed the excited woman. "August is too good a man to marry his Swan woman, and my husband and I want him with us."

Christina was not present in the Court, and for fear August would again try to escape from her, Justice White held Morio until to-day, when he will see that the couple are married. August is only eighteen years old, but is an experienced workman. His brother is a shoemaker, and business being dull he finds it hard to support his wife without August's assistance.

August, married at eighteen against his will, by the magistrate of a republic, may rub his eyes and fancy hir .

self back in Germany, under an even more paternal *régime* than he knew there. When we read of Frederick the Great going about Berlin, berating the apple-women who did not knit as they sat at their stalls, or flogging other idlers with his cane, we may admire the energy and watchfulness of the old man without admitting the divine right of kings to administer personal chastisement at discretion. So, too, we may admire the official benevolence that would ease the heartache of Christina, or save from potential harm the gambler's wife, without admitting the right of republics to arrest people *ad libitum.* It is common to place witnesses under arrest in free America; and a judge in New Jersey assures me that the thief who steals my watch may be bailed out of jail, while I am held in durance vile as a witness against him ! *

The American's motto is "hurry up;" he applies it to every transaction of his life. He skips half the marriage-service, and leaves out the long prayers at funerals. In his legal affairs he is equally quick. It is handier when you have your man, be he witness or offender, to clap him into jail than to go through the trouble of taking his name and address, and serving at his house a magistrate's summons. Such things may do for an old effete monarchy; but in the new republic things have

---

* " We have frequently called attention to the inconsistency of the law which allows a ·person charged with crime to remain at large and locks up in prison an innocent witness to the offence. Not long ago a man who was arrested for assaulting a woman he was alleged to have enticed into his house was liberated on bail, while his victim was held a close prisoner in the House of Detention until the trial took place."—*The New York World,* June 21, 1887

to "hurry up," and individual rights often get jostled in the rush. Remember, America is five hours behind England, and men have to put in all they know to make up those five hours. A New Yorker who gets a splash of oil on his hat when passing under the elevated railway simply runs into the nearest hatter's and buys a new tile. An Englishman would spend several weeks waiting about the law courts, and pay two or three pounds in lawyer's fees, in order to make the railway company pay for the damaged hat.

As a rule the Englishman is phlegmatic and cold-blooded; but if the incident described in the following extract had happened in Berkeley Square or Porchester Terrace, there would have been a small revolution :

" A small regiment of Italian laborers, with picks and shovels on their shoulders, marched noiselessly into Thirty-fourth street, between Fifth and Sixth avenues, just as darkness was setting in on Wednesday. A moment later the aristocratic quiet of the street was broken by the sharp contact of steel picks with Belgian blocks. Toil-hardened hands rapidly piled the blocks into long heaps on the south sidewalk, and mounds of dirt looking like miniature mountain ranges sprang up in the street. One by one the doors of the fine houses in the street were opened, and floods of light streamed out with indignant citizens, who demanded from the foreman of the laborers what authority he had for digging up the street. The foreman showed a permit from the Department of Public Works, and introduced the indignant citizens to Inspector Mooney. The permit allowed the Thirty-fourth Street Railroad Construction Company to lay tracks in Thirty-fourth street. The road got the consent of the Board of Aldermen several months ago. The indignant citizens denounced the work as an outrage, and hurried around among their friends and neighbors asking and making suggestions as to what they ought to do. They finally concluded that, as the courts were closed then, they would have to wait. So they all went to their homes and tried to

sleep. They were unable to do this, however, as, in addition to
the sound of picks and shovels and the clatter of Belgian blocks,
they heard the buzz of the cross-cut saw going through joists and
sleepers and the jangle of steel rails on the stones. At midnight
the noise ceased, and the laborers shouldered their implements and
marched away."

In this instance the residents took such a vigorous
course that the rails were taken up and the road is still
clear. But in the case of Forty-second Street the people
were powerless to prevent the laying of the tracks; and
the jingle of the carbells now sounds night and day
through this once-fashionable street. Such occasional
awakenings are good for the New Yorkers. They serve
to divert their attention from business to local politics,
and remind them of the class of men they are governed
by. They serve also to show the true character of the
political fetish from which, by some kind of Mumbo-
Jumboism, they expect to get "the greatest happiness
of the greatest number."

The history of social progress is the history of the
emancipation from tyranny. In America and in England, the individual has freed himself from the tyranny
of nobles, kings and other species of despots; but he is
now being enslaved by a new oppressor—the will of the
majority. The old Grecian theory that the individual
has no rights against the State has been rehabilitated
by modern politicians; and in the two foremost countries of the world, the proposition has acquired the
reputation of an axiom. "The greatest good of the
greatest number" is an admirable thing to legislate for;
but when every man differs from every other man as to
what really is the greatest good, and as to what really is

the best means of achieving it, the crystallization of opinions into laws is apt to display irregularities, causing flaws, fractures and failures of all kinds. There never was a time when political theorizing was carried to such an extreme as at present, nor a time when more good and thoughtful men were working out what they think is the political salvation of the race. But unity of opinion amongst these workers does not exist. There is no common political creed. All are dissenters—except in one particular, and here all are agreed. Socialists, anarchists, communists, land-nationalizationists, protectionists—all agree that the individual has no rights against the State. And in conformity with this belief, law-makers are at work in parliament, in congress, and

State legislature, creating greater happiness for greater numbers by depriving the units of the power of making themselves happy in their own fashion. In short, there is being created a type of citizen wholly without self-dependence—one who lacks initiative, and who constantly expects government to do things that ought to be done by himself. Human nature is plastic and lends itself readily to legis-

Legislator modelling a citizen.

lative moulding. It is a questionable kindness of the law-maker, however, to fashion the citizen after the model of a mendicant.

The affectionate cruelty of governmental methods re-

minds one of Isaac Walton's funny directions for fishing
with frogs. Says he: "Thus use your
frog: put your hook, I mean the arming wire, through his mouth, and out
at his gills, and then with a fine needle
and silk sew the upper part of his leg
with only one stitch to the arming wire
of your hook, or tie the frog's leg above
the upper joint to the armed wire; and
in so doing, use him *as though you loved him*"!

The modern legislator is the angler. Lovingly,
gently, firmly he takes the citizen for bait, passes a
hook through his gills, sews him up with a fine needle
and the prettiest colored silk, or ties his hands to his
feet with red tape, and affectionately dangling him into
the stream of human perplexities, waits for the greatest
happiness of the greatest number. Atavism? Atavism
is much too good a name for it!

There is much laudation of direct methods nowadays. If you see an evil, go for it! Go for it by the
shortest cut! In Felkin's *Uganda* there is a funny
story of a direct method:

"We went one day," says he, "to pay a visit to a [Soudanese]
officer, and to our surprise found him lying on a bed with his
head hanging over the end of it, having a small paper funnel
stuck into one nostril, and at the same time chewing something.
On our asking the meaning of this extraordinary proceeding, he
replied that he was suffering from headache, and wished to grease
his brain, so was pouring oil down the funnel into his nose, under
the impression that it would find its way into the skull; and he
said, pointing to his temple, 'You see, if I chew at the same time,
it makes the brain work, so that it will be more quickly greased.'" *

* ii. 160.

This is the kind of pathology legislators practise when Society's head aches. To alleviate pain in the body politic this is the order of intelligence used, the quality of scientific knowledge displayed. And yet, forsooth, men speak of the government as they speak of Wisdom, Justice, or any other abstraction, forgetting that "the Government" is but Some-of-us elected to *serve* All-of-us. So completely are men dominated by this government superstition that one rarely hears condemnation of a stupid meddlesome law; they accept it as natural and inevitable, as they would bad crops or a tornado. A man who had legislatures at his beck and call is reputed to have said: "The public be damned!" It is nearly time for the public to reverse this saying on the government both in England and America, even with a rumbling double-bass accompaniment from anarchists and nihilists.

CHAPTER VIII.

CITIES AND SOCIAL SETS.

"In men this blunder still you find,
All think their little set mankind."

HANNAH MORE.

"WHO was the first man?" asked a teacher of his class. "George Washington!" promptly replied a bright-eyed boy; adding in an undertone the oftquoted lines —"First in peace, first in war, and first in the hearts of his countrymen!" "But did you never hear of Adam?" queried the surprised teacher. "Oh yes, *but he was a foreigner.*"

Concerning national institutions—and George Washington is one—the American people display complete unanimity of feeling. This bright boy's answer is one

that might have been given in any schoolhouse between
Kennebunkport in Maine and Kewaskum in Wisconsin.
On the general excellence of the United States as a nation, or of America as a continent, no difference of opinion exists from the Atlantic to the Pacific, or, as our
friend of the Paris dinner-party would say, from the Aurora Borealis in the north to the precession of the equinoxes in the south.   Indeed it is only by a supreme effort
that politicians can get up any difference of opinion on
questions of national policy.   Parties like our conserva-
tives and liberals with strong dividing lines, are unknown
in America; the nearest approach to them being the tariff-
reform party, generally identified with the democrats,
and the iron-bound protectionists, led by a few prominent republicans.   Except on this question, Americans
are unanimous that as a nation they have nothing to desire, nothing to amend, modify or reform.   As a result
nobody takes any interest in the doings of Congress—
except in the periodical discussions of the silver question and the tariff.   The governmental machine is perfect and automatic; and so it is allowed to run along
without the constant jolting and frequent stoppages of
older machines with their intricate equipment of cabi-
nets, executives, oppositions and the like.

But with perfect unanimity about things national
there goes complete dissent about things civic.   The
rivalries of cities are carried to a ludicrous extreme.
The Philadelphian has nothing favourable to say of
the Bostonian; and both agree that no good can come
from Gotham.   While Chicago hates St. Louis with a
hatred that is qualified only by the pride of having sur-
passed her, she is willing to agree with her quondam
rival in despising Detroit or Milwaukee.   Minneapolis
and St. Paul, originally situated a dozen miles apart,

now mingle their suburbs, and hate each other worse
than Sparta detested Athens. Each charges the other
with copying into the census names from tombstones,
and duplicating living citizens, so as to appear greater
than its rival; and it is averred that young men living
in either city marry by preference girls belonging to
the rival city, so as to decrease its population by one!
These towns will awake some morning to find themselves wards of a greater city than either has yet
dreamed of.

This rivalry takes a strong hold of journalists, and
newspapers are made spicy with quips and quirks about
neighbouring cities. In a list of recipes to keep cool
with a ninety-nine thermometer given in *Life,* two are
jokes aimed at rival cities. One way to keep cool is to
"talk to a Boston girl;" another is to "go to Philadelphia." Bostonians say that people often die in Philadelphia of sheer inanition—the place is so dull; and it
is asserted that strangers visiting the Quaker City and
going into society are literally bored to death. Philadel-
phians retort with stories about the Boston girl, or re-
late how cows coming home with dreary windings, laid out
Boston streets, and
gave them that crook-
edness which is so re-
freshing after life in
cities built in geomet-
ric figures. "But
you will admit that
our city is at least
well laid out," said a
Philadelphia girl at
Bar Harbor, playing

"Well laid out."

her last trump in a game with one of the elect from Bos-

ton. "Well laid out? Oh yes; but Boston would be
better laid out if it were only half as dead!" and she
calmly wrote "Hub" on the sands. It really seems that
Philadelphia always gets the worst of these contests; and
the result is that she is more subject to attack than any
other city. This was neatly expressed by a young lady
from Cincinnati with whom I was talking at Washington. I was saying that Philadelphia was a city of homes,
not of apartment-houses: "it spread over a far greater
area than New York with less than half the inhabitants."
"That's because it has been so much sat upon," promptly
replied the fair Cincinnatian. I once innocently asked
a lady from Detroit what sort of a place was Kalamazoo.
"Oh," said she, with ineffable scorn, "Kalamazoo is a
little one-horse place where they raise celery and have a
lunatic asylum." The imputation of large feet to Chicago and St. Louis girls by other cities is another outcome of this rivalry; but this, the girls of St. Louis protest, is "carrying a joke to extremities." I lately read
in an Eastern journal that railway conductors now an-
nounce the arrival of the train by crying "Chicago!
twenty minutes for divorce!" But Chicago rarely "gets
left" in this kind of banter. A stranger visiting the
Garden City went to the theatre, and thinking he would
get a better seat if the clerk in the box-office knew that
he represented a great community, said: "I come from
Boston." "Boston!" repeated the clerk as though he
imperfectly remembered the name; "is not that the
place where they spell 'culture' with a big C and 'God'
with a little g?"

Americans cry "Chestnuts!" when they hear the beginning of an old story. Englishmen wait to the end,
and then with a smile say: "I always liked that story."

It is hard to say which is the more discouraging; but I am willing to risk both in the hope of occasionally giving a new form to an old joke or telling an old story to a new hearer.

Much has been written by English excursionists to the United States in deprecation of the custom of naming towns after historic places in the old world. If the excursionists stayed long enough they would outgrow this feeling. Babylon on Long Island has the pleasantest of memories for me; and I know some excellent men of whom I am agreeably reminded by the names of their homes at Syracuse, Utica and Goshen. The index to stations in an American railway-guide is one of the funniest bits of reading—after Johnson's dictionary—that a picnic party ever indulged in. Mixed up with names such as Nazareth, Jericho, Rome, Carthage, are Indian names such as Koshkonong, Ty-Ty, Wahkiakum, Snohomish, or Klikatat. Then there are samples of native ingenuity like Hookium, Nenolepops, Lick-skillet, Hog-eye, Shirttail Bend, Puppytown, Squitch Gulch, Toenail Lake, and an infinity of Smithopolises, Jonesopolises, or Robinsonvilles!

At our picnic "Manly Junction" raised the suggestion that it be changed to "Gentlemanly Junction"—as sounding better; while the name of a California town recalled a story which the lady who told it said was a very naughty one. It was of a man, who having asked a demure-looking girl, a small boy and a sad-eyed clergyman, "What town is this?" concluded from their answers that the whole population was vulgar, rude, and addicted to profanity. The town was Yuba Dam. Nineveh, Athens, Corinth, Memphis, Cairo, are represented on the American continent, some by "little one-horse places" as my Detroit friend would say; some by towns surpassing in size and wealth their historic proto-types. One would naturally think that the association of such names with little dingy towns of unpainted wooden houses and plastic roads, would deprive Americans of that mingled reverence and awe which old places and historic names inspire in us. But no such effect is seen in Americans abroad. Indeed their delight in historic places is greater than that of those who live surrounded by the evidences of past ages and generations of men. An American after visiting London usually knows more of the haunts of Johnson, Goldsmith, Dickens and other writers whom he has known since boyhood, than does the native Londoner, to whom Fleet Street is peopled with active business rivals rather than with the spirits of departed authors.

American cities usually have some nickname, derived from their most striking peculiarities. Brooklyn—called after Breukelen, a little village near Utrecht—is the City of Churches. Gotham is an old nickname for New York which is sinking into forgetfulness. In old files of newspapers I have seen many a laugh at the Gothamites. Still " I ween that more fools pass through Gotham than remain in it," for it is a delightful city. Washington, laid out on paper as an immense city, remains the City of Magnificent Distances, though it is rapidly fulfilling the great expectations entertained of it. Chicago is prettily called the Garden City; but it has a rival for this name in the toy city built on Long Island by Stewart the millionaire haberdasher. Boston, besides being the Hub of the Universe, disputes with Edinburgh the name of Modern Athens. Mushroomopolis is the awkward-sounding cognomination which Kansas City has earned by its rapid growth. Cincinnati is called by residents Queen City. Non-residents and scoffers used to call it Porkopolis; but Chicago has deprived it of its claim to this as first pig-sticking city in America. Duluth while it was a city mainly on paper and laid out in the backwoods, became the "Zenith City of the Unsalted Seas," and its growth from almost nothing to thirty thousand in fifteen years justifies some such appellation.

The rivalries of Italian cities in mediæval times have rarely given origin to a more romantic story than that of Duluth's contest with its quondam rival Superior, concerning the canal across Minnesota Point. The Northern Pacific Railway made Duluth its lake terminus, but soon experienced inconvenience because it had no harbour save the shallow upper end of the Bay of Superior. Fearing that the railway people would move their terminus, the citizens of Duluth decided to make a canal across the narrow sandspit of Minnesota Point, so as to connect their harbour directly with the lake. But the town of Superior, which occupied a position at the mouth of the bay, alleged that the waters of the St. Louis River would leave their natural channel through the bay and flow out through the canal, if it were made, leaving their town high and dry; and they made such representations to the government that an injunction was granted forbidding the canal. The lawyers had to go for their injunction to Topeka, Kansas, where the United States Circuit Court was sitting. The news was telegraphed to enterprising Duluth, and while the papers were speeding northward in the train, the canal was commenced. Every man, woman, and child in Duluth who could handle a spade or shovel, or beg, borrow or steal a bucket or basket, flocked down to the point, and dug, scratched, burrowed at the canal until it was finished. Before the lawyers reached the Zenith City of the Unsalted Seas, the citizens and their wives and children were celebrating the accomplishment of their great work. The result predicted by Superior followed: a strong current set out through the canal, and the old entrance to the bay shallowed three feet in the next gale. Rivalry between the two towns has now ceased. Superior belies her name and remains the village she has been for a quarter of a century. Duluth is great and prosperous. Wharves and grain-elevators are springing up on her sandy point; and a busy commercial centre has leaped into existence. A dozen short lines centre there already, and six great railways will soon be pouring into Duluth, the vast commercial drainage of the great northwest. Bravo, Duluth!

The society of each town is not homogeneous. There are strata in republican society just as there are in

aristocratic communities. But a man is not born into a rank, and taught by the catechism to remain there : to do his duty in that state of life to which it has pleased God to call him. In America, he passes up and down, though with some limi-

tations. His position is often regulated by his balance at the bank. At other times the nature of his business indicates his social peg-hole. The society of Cincinnati, for example, was found by a Bostonian to be divided into Stick-'ems and Stuck-'ems. The former class consisted of those who still stick pigs; the latter was made up of those who have stuck 'em, but who stick 'em no longer: retired pork-packers—not butchers —and their children. Similarly in Pittsburgh, I was told by a resident that one's father must own a blast-furnace to secure one's admission to the ultra-fashionable set. The grade immediately beneath this, I was told, was formed by those whose fathers had ceased to work in shirt-sleeves. It was a Pittsburgher, by the way, who said that in America there are only three generations from shirt-sleeves to shirt-sleeves. In Washington the society is mainly political, and the grades are there formed by ministers, senators and congressmen. Except among the ladies there is little attention paid to rules of precedence. American men have no time for such nonsense. In Philadelphia a few old Quaker families who do not go much into society, monopolize the glamour that ancient birth confers. For the rest, the society is commercial, the strata being those common in England, of which the most conspicuous are the "retail" and the "wholesale." New York is a cosmopolitan city. Indeed Chicagoans deny that it is American. An Irishman landing there cries, "Be dad! it's fur all the wurrld loike Corrk!" A German exclaims, *Ganz wie Berlin;* the Chicagoan bluntly asks: "What's the next train for the United States?" The society of New York may not be representative of American society in general; but it is very enjoyable. After London, New York! After New York, the Del—I mean Boston! In the Empire City the social strata are not horizontal and superposed, but vertical and side by side. There are many "sets," but it would be difficult to indicate the highest. Perhaps the one which is all-powerful in Boston and which is pretty large in New York, should be named first, the intellectual set.   The nucleus of this is formed by the Nineteenth Century Club, a society of some hundred and fifty members of both sexes, before whom every conceivable subject from Christian dogma to Free Love is discussed without fastidiousness and yet with sensibility.   It is a curious amalgam of fashion and intellect.   Its meetings take the form of social receptions held until lately at the house of the president in Gramercy Park, now at the art-galleries in Madison Square.   Writers of repute from other cities and members of the club read papers or make speeches on all conceivable topics, while the members and their friends to the number of about five hundred sit around on camp-chairs in all the glory of swallow-tails and décolleté

Discussing the lecture.

dresses.   Here intellectual gems vie in brilliancy with diamond bracelets, and shapely necks and heaving bosoms divide your attention with glowing thoughts and well-turned phrases.   It is a heavenly combination!   The club has no constitution.   Its motto, "Prove all things; hold fast that which is good," indicates the width of its hearth. Round it in friendly converse, gather Catholic priests, Unitarian and Baptist ministers, Free-thinkers, Agnostics, Positivists, Socialists, Cremationists, and thinkers of every possible type, but always of good calibre. It is indeed a microcosm of the world—except that grumblers are excluded. I never heard of any similar society in which envy, hatred, malice and all uncharitableness were so conspicuously absent. Neither are there any of those little jealousies which make up the irritants of life. Round this centre of light, gyrate smaller social systems, with all their attendant orbs and satellites, spreading far across space—from Madison Square to Harlem and Hoboken—and dotting the intellectual firmament with an infinitude of lesser lights.

Next should be mentioned the Knickerbockers—the descendants of the Dutch squatters of New Amsterdam before the British took it and called it New York. These are hardly to be called a set. Though proud of their lineage they are not at all exclusive, and may be found in every circle. Their old Dutch names have rarely been anglicized, as is often the case with French and German names, and in the New York directory may be found such jaw-dislocators as have been strung together in the following rhyme:

A Dutch squatter.

" Where be the Dutchmen of the olden time,
   Who saw our ancient city in its prime?
   The Vander Voots, Van Rippers, and Dycks;
   The Vanderheydens, Slingerlands, Ten Eycks;
   The Knickerbockers, Lansings, and Van Burens,
   Van Dams, Van Winkles, Stuyvesants, Van Kewrens;

The Hoffmans, Rosbooms, Hogebooms and Schroders,
Van Valkenburghs, and Stoutenburghs and Schneiders,
Van Schaacks, Van Vechtens, Visschers, and Van Wies,
Van Tromps, Van Schoonhovens, and Vanderzees,
Van Zandts, Van Clarcoms, Schuylers, Van Schellynes,
Douws, Hooglands, Waldrons, Vanderburghs, and Pruyns.
De Witts, Hochstrasses, Bontecous, Van Gicsons,
Van Gaasbecks, Grosbecks, Bensons, Van and Hiesons:
Where are they all, those men of sounding name,
Of pipe, knee-breeches and round-bellied frame?"

The authors and artists of New York have their clubs,
but they form no set. Their periodical meetings are
merry gatherings of the free-and-easy kind; and here
one may learn that great men can drop their dignity,
and revel in lager beer and chipped beef like ordinary
mortals. The Century Club is the Athenæum of
America. It has a very stately look after the Author's
Club. The Lotus corresponds nearest to our Savage.
The brightest of Bohemians make this their resting-
place.

One hears in New York of a small set of ultra-fashion-
ables, who are said to be so exclusive that it is only by
reading the social items in the *Home Journal* or the
World that one can know what is going on in it. This
set consists of the few to whom wealth has survived
descent through two generations. I have met several
members of this circle. There is nothing remarkable to
report about them. They incline to ape the British
aristocracy; and of this their exclusiveness is quoted as
a sign. Some members of this set were, a few years ago,
publicly rebuked by the director of the opera for loud
talking during the performance. It takes more than
three generations for some natures to get accustomed to
wealth.

This reminds one of the great change which has taken place in American manners since Mrs. Trollope's day. Mrs. Trollope wrote her impressions of America fifty years ago, and, joined with some exaggeration, told so many unpleasant truths that her name in American mouths has not yet recovered its naturally sweet savour. One of the truths she told was that at the theatres of certain western cities, men were in the habit of taking off their coats during the performance, and sitting on the front of the boxes with their backs to the people. In consequence of this criticism, the manners of theatre-goers were much improved; and it became usual for the audience to cry " Trollope! Trollope!" at any man who took his coat off during the performance, sat on the edge of the box with his back to the people, or otherwise publicly misbehaved himself. In the newspapers of fifty years ago I have several times read of this cry of " Trollope! Trollope!"

Nowadays Americans are much more careful to avoid little rudenesses than Englishmen. Indeed, the positions are reversed on the wandering Briton, who can invariably be known by his remaining covered in places where Americans always remove their hats. It may not be amiss, and is certainly not superfluous, to tell Englishmen who intend to visit America that it is the custom to remove the hat in any building where ladies are. This applies especially to an elevator, and the passages and halls of a hotel. Another much-needed hint to Englishmen abroad is, " Don't grumble *very* much— aloud!" I once saw a party of Englishmen, directors of a Canadian Railway, enter the dining-room of the Windsor Hotel with a greater clatter than the advent of a great Bashaw. They loudly insisted on having a particular table, though told that it was reserved for a family that had lived in the hotel for many years; and when they finally did get seated, nothing appeared to give them satisfaction. A man who will grumble at the table of the Windsor Hotel will complain about the fit of the heavenly halo, or say that his cloud-throne in Paradise is damp!

CHAPTER IX.

A MODERN RACE OF CYCLOPS.

Cyclops, "an insolent lawless race"—
"giants with only one eye."—WEBSTER.

WHEN Herbert Spencer was in America, his experience of journalists reminded him of a witticism of the poet Heine: "When a woman writes a novel, she has one eye on the paper and the other on some man—except the Countess Hahn-Hahn, who has only one eye." In American journals everything is treated in connection with the doings of individuals. The leader-writer, discussing some question of state, has one eye on the governmental department, and the other on the person who presides over the department. If he has only one eye, he fixes it on the person. It was such a one-eyed journalist who, a week or two after the inauguration of President Cleveland, expressed his indignation in the *Galveston News* because a salute was fired at Fortress Monroe "in honor of Mr. Chester Arthur, a New York attorney."

The small invasions of personal liberty to which one is often subject in the freedom-loving Republic take a specially aggressive form when conducted by journalists. A citizen is practically without rights when confronted by a reporter. If his daughter or his wife elopes, if his house takes fire, if the bank breaks with his savings, or his son absconds to Canada with the property of trustful clients, the interviewer, who has the effrontery of a brass sign and the persistence of a Nasmyth hammer, stands before the victim note-book in hand ere he has time to estimate his misfortune. Like the holy inquisitors of mediæval times, this child of freedom scruples not to torture his victim, worming out his secrets, and quietly menacing him with unnamed terrors until he is ready to cry:

> O God, defend me! how am I beset—
> What kind of catechising call you this?

Nothing is so grateful to the interviewer as scandal. He thrives in it like eels in mud. He revels and rolls in it until it covers him like a coating of slime, obscuring every vestige of the man. He often inflicts cruelty to see his victim writhe, that he may turn an honest penny by describing the agony he causes. In pursuit of newsy items he adds to persistence a quality which in nobler walks of life would be called courage: it is the courage of the flea that fears not to breakfast on the lip of a lion. If he is kicked down the front steps he crawls back by the area window and cross-examines the cook. I know of a case where he got into a house by a back window and refused to leave until his coat-tails had been covered with foot-marks. Every man's house is his castle; but the sheriff, the plague, and the interviewer have rights of entry that will not brook denial.

English readers lately learnt something about interviewing from a controversy between Mr. Russell Lowell and Mr. Julian Hawthorne. In America the incident induced a discussion of this form of social aggression which has not been without its good results. The *Nation* probably stands at the head of American journalism, for the integrity as well as ability with which it is conducted. Here is its contribution to the discussion:

" The Boston *Herald* says that the assertion that there is 'a very large body' of newspaper men who would be guilty of Hawthorne's offence may be true of New York, but not of Boston, where 'any newspaper man who did what Mr. Lowell says Mr. Hawthorne did to him would lose his place and stand a poor chance of getting another.' The Springfield *Republican* goes further, and says the number of newspaper men anywhere who would commit Hawthorne's offence is not large, but small. There is no use in continuing or carrying on a controversy on a point which in the nature of things cannot be decided. But we will say this, that in long experience of the newspaper press we have known of scores, if not hundreds, of most shameful and cruel violations of confidence and intrusions on privacy committed by newspaper men, and have never heard of one which led to the dismissal of the offender, if it was one which promoted ' sales,' or, in other words, brought money into the counting room. Small lies or outrages, which have no particular pecuniary value, are sometimes followed by punishment, but it is a well-known fact that managers are very apt to stand by, to the last extremity, a liar whose lies feed the popular appetite for amusement. This is not a pleasant thing to say about ' our profession,' but it is as true as gospel. As a matter of fact, some of the most highly paid newspaper men are notorious liars, perverters, and inventors."

It is one of the tokens of a free country that your sixteen-year-old daughter may go out to post a letter, and come back in ten minutes to tell you that she has just married your errand-boy or your footman. While you are tearing your hair and committing free institutions to Sheol, a bit of pasteboard is thrust in your hand announcing the interviewer. You then get another lesson in freedom. Your domestic suffering is claimed by the nation, which wants to gossip over your calamity. Here is an example extracted from the *New York Tribune* for March 24, 1885. I omit the name of the sufferer, who was one of the best-known men in New York:

" The bride's father was found in his apartments at No. —— Broadway.

' Mr. ——,' said the reporter, ' to morrow's issue of *The Tribune* will contain—'

' I know,' interrupted Mr. ——, ' a notice of my daughter's marriage. Suppress it—suppress it if possible! '

The reporter explained that such things cannot be suppressed, and Mr. —— continued: ' I suppose you want to know all about it, but, I implore you, make as little of a sensation out of the affair as the facts will allow. I have always tried to appear honorably before the public, and now this comes upon me with the suddenness of a thunderbolt. You can't imagine what a blow the marriage has been to me,' continued he in a voice from which the tears were not far distant. ' I know that my position will remain the same, but I can't bear that my daughter should destroy her happiness by a single rash step like this. The whole story, however, is simple, and has really no sensational elements. My daughter made the acquaintance of this young man in this city. He didn't dare to pay his attentions openly, for he knew how I would have regarded them. He met her out of my house and they got married. I can't give you any further particulars. I know absolutely nothing about the young man, but I'm doing all I can to find out about him. That's my present occupation. The marriage service was performed by a clergyman regularly ordained, and I never knew of the matter until the other day.' "

Here is an interviewer's horror extracted from the *Philadelphia Press,* which like the *Tribune* is a first-class paper, judged by the American standard. I omit the victim's name, which the journalist had not the heart to conceal:

" As they were entering the hearing-room [of the police station] the Sergeant said: 'There is a case for you,' pointing to a woman who was speaking to the turnkey. She was a sad specimen of a dissipated woman. Ragged, filthy and half drunk, she stood, asking for a lodging, without any shawl to protect her emaciated form, or hood to cover her unkempt gray locks that fell down her back.

'You would hardly believe,' whispered the Sergeant, 'that fifteen years ago that creature was a beautiful young woman, well educated, the daughter of wealthy parents moving in the best society in Chicago.'

The reporter looked incredulous.

'Well, she was,' replied the Sergeant. 'Her father, whose name was W——, was one of the richest men in that city, and lost all he had, along with his life, in the great fire. Just a few weeks previously, however, his daughter, our visitor here, was married to a man named R——. He only wanted her money, and deserted her at the discovery of her father's loss.'

The turnkey was heard gruffly to answer 'Yes,' and pointed to the stairway. As she turned around she showed a face wrinkled and grimy, with eyes half closed from drunken stupidity. Grasping the front of her dress that dragged on the floor, she swayed toward the door.

'Mrs. R——,' said the reporter, politely, as she was about to pass.

At the sound of the name she suddenly turned, her face losing its despair, and stood like a statue, staring at the speaker like one in a dream. Finally recovering herself, she grasped the reporter's arm convulsively, and looking up in his face appealingly, said in a husky voice: 'Who—who are you? Do you know me?' She turned her head and murmured: 'O God, that I should come to this!'

'I am very, very sorry, indeed, to see you here. How did it happen?'

The tears gathered in her eyes and she began to sob violently. 'Oh, I could not help it,' she said, shaking her head. 'When my husband deserted me so cruelly after my father's death, I tried to live respectably, but I couldn't find work, and I had learned to drink before my father died. My only hope now is in the grave.'

With her face buried in her hands and the tears trickling through her fingers, she slowly walked toward the stairway and disappeared, as though anxious to hide her misery.

'We often have people among our lodgers who've seen better days,' commented the Sergeant. 'We get used to them. That poor creature to-morrow will be about the low saloons trying to raise enough to buy a glass of rum.' "

I am aware that a stranger's denunciation of this system will occasion some resentment in America, especially among journalists. But I trust I have shown myself sufficiently in sympathy with what is admirable in the Republic to excuse condemnation of what is clearly a lapse from higher to lower forms. In Russia every family is under government surveillance; in the Republic of America every person is liable to forms of espionage far more objectionable. And this is both demanded and conceded as a right to the press. "The reporter explained that such things cannot be suppressed"! And why not? The sanctity of home, the feelings of the wretched parents, the future happiness even of the foolish couple—are all to be subordinated to an unworthy craving for gossip? It is a saying in America that personal rights must give way to public comfort; but surely the public amusement is not included.

Then by what right, republican, Christian or other, does a reporter interview the occupant of a prison-cell?

Has a drunkard no rights? Is he (or she, alas! in this case) to be exhibited to needy penny-a-liners as stock in trade? If this wretched interviewer must live—and I see no need for it—is it the duty of public officials to cater to him? But the subject is too nauseating. That such things happen without exciting surprise or protest is ample proof, if other proofs were not abundant, that

Americans lack that respect for the rights of others which ought to go along with insistence on their own.

But perhaps the interview in jail is one of those dismal little fictions with which American editors sometimes beguile their readers. The *New York Herald* once startled the city by reporting the escape of the wild animals from Central Park. The horrible scenes that ensued were described: nurses were killed, children devoured or torn in pieces, and the people about the park were afraid to move out. Many did not read to the end of the report; those who did found the statement that it was all a dream or something of the kind!

President Cleveland lately said:

"I don't think that there ever was a time when newspaper lying was so general and so mean as at present, and there never was a country under the sun where it flourished as it does in this. The falsehoods daily spread before the people in our newspapers, while they are proofs of the mental ingenuity of those engaged in newspaper work, are insults to the American love for decency and fair play of which we boast."

9

Speaking of this indictment, the *Tribune*, a rabidly partisan newspaper, capable of ascribing a tornado in Texas or a collision of ferry-boats to democratic jobbery, makes the following very suggestive comment:

" As the President is generally credited with sincerity and good intentions, it is evident that his acrid strictures upon the American press are designed to serve some useful purpose. We take it that his criticisms are meant largely for the benefit of the democratic press, which aided in electing him in a campaign of reckless and malevolent defamation unparalleled in the political annals of the country. His opponent was attacked month after month as no statesman in American public life had ever been assailed before. Mr. Blaine's correspondence was monstrously perverted, his private business transactions were ransacked with malign purpose, and the sanctity of his home wantonly invaded. From beginning to end it was a campaign of malignant defamation on the part of the democratic press."

But "from beginning to end it was a campaign of malignant defamation on the part of the republican press" as well, and of malignant defamation the *Tribune* was not altogether innocent. Indeed then, as ever since, this otherwise able journal has shown a pitiful lack of dignity in its criticisms of the democratic party. Its unreasoning malevolence must inevitably discredit its own party in the minds of all lovers of fair play.

It will scarcely be credited in England that fictitious interviews are published by reputable newspapers, in which full names are given. While I write, such a fabrication concerning the inventor Edison is going the rounds of the press, having already appeared in dailies published in Washington, Philadelphia and New York. The article is extravagant and absurd to the last degree, being founded on an old hoax which I am informed appeared as an April-fool joke nine years ago.

I have found in a California paper an amusing report of a menagerie catastrophe, evidently prompted by the *Herald's* horror. It is a good example of a kind of humour which Uncle Sam has made his own, and worth quoting:

"Cooper and Bailey's menagerie, which will open in this city shortly, was the scene of a terrifying occurrence, while exhibiting at Marysville recently. It seems that some mischievous youngster in the audience inserted a piece of tobacco in a peanut given by him to the largest of the sixteen elephants attached to the show. The enraged creature uttered the singular half-human cry peculiar to its species when aroused, and hurled the boy with great force through the roof of the tent, breaking every bone in his body, and an almost new humming-top in his pocket. Bursting the ten-inch chain that secured its foot like a bit of twine, the furious mammoth seized the clown, and in a second had crushed him into a shapeless pulp and old conundrums. The elephant's companions now became excited, and charged upon the audience, which was wildly applauding the clown's just fate, little thinking what was in store for itself. In a twinkling the ring-master had been disposed of, and the first four rows of spectators had become a mass of writhing victims. The ring ran with gore, and the wild shrieks and roars of the other animals lent additional horror to the terrible scene. Presently, several cages were upset in the mêlée, and the lions and tigers took part in the awful fray. The hippopotamus bit off the sheriff's head. A frightful contest occurred between the grizzly bear and one of the largest elephants. The latter was underneath, and in his struggles rolled over and smashed flat a whole half-priced Sunday-school. The rhinoceros paid exclusive attention to the deadhead seats, and at one time was noticed with two editors and a politician on the same horn. The camels and zebras tore round the ring, uttering terrific cries, above which could be faintly heard the agonizing cries of the County Recorder, who was being skinned alive by a couple of gorillas on top of the centre pole. In course of time the carnage was quelled, and the animals and curiosities secured, with the exception of a cormorant, that will go practising law in the spring, if not detected in time. The remains of the Mayor and six Councilmen were sent home in the golden chariot (cost $40,000 to build), preceded by the band (seventy-four first class soloists). The unrecognized dead were buried in a trench two hundred feet long. The animals are now secured by chains weighing four pounds to the link, and iron bars two feet thick. Owing to the colossal expense attendant upon this mammoth exhibition of the century, the price of admission has been reduced to fifty cents, children under ten half price."

In the picturesque American neology, a "deadhead" means a person with a free pass.

Sensational titles to reports are the delight of the American editor. A leading Chicago paper paid a large salary to an alliterative genius who did nothing but concoct head-lines. This fellow once had to give a heading to the description of an execution; and next morning subscribers were startled on opening their papers to see in large capitals the words "Jerked to Jesus." This is a fact, however shocking it may be. Another heading to a similar account which I have seen is "Leaped into Eternity." This was the description of a public hanging in a field near Savannah on June 26, 1885. The reporter ended his description with these words: "The widow of the murdered man occupied a seat on the scaffold, and witnessed her husband's assassin take his leap into eternity."

It is not easy to think of the American press as a serious institution. What it looks like to a native it is hard to say; but to a stranger it appears a gigantic farce, understood as such by both writers and readers. Everybody in America reads the newspapers; nobody seems to believe them. Indeed it is often asked in a quizzical

way: "Is it true, or did you read it in a newspaper?" For
nearly a week after the presidential election, republican
newspapers, led by the *Tribune*, solemnly assured readers that Mr. Blaine had been elected. Rarely is the
love of truth allowed to spoil a fine sentence. In this
particular the American journalist is like Carlyle: if his
nicely-rounded period happens to exaggerate the facts,
so much the worse for the facts. If you read that "the
awful holocaust leaped with lurid hands to lick the em-
blazoned clouds that caught the irradiant glare and hurled
it into the abysmal spaces beyond the paling star," you
may be certain, without reading another line, that a cow-
barn, worth three hundred dollars, has been burnt down.
When General Scott, the conqueror of Mexico, visited
his native village in Pennsylvania, his entrance into the
place was thus described by the local editor: "The gallant
hero, seated in a chariot, led the van. The rosy morn
besprinkled the oriental clouds with effulgent glory, and
the gorgeous sun, at last issuing like a warrior from his
repose, walked up the sky, gilding the vast expanse of
ether, and throwing his broad and splendid rays upon a
line of one-horse wagons and carts filled with individuals
principally from our village."

I have already quoted the saying of a newspaper man
to the effect that all American journalists are liars—
either liars on space or liars on salary. This statement
coming from a journalist must also be untrue. And
here is a dilemma I will leave to the newspapers. But
Thomas Jefferson writing in 1807 shows that the complaint of President Cleveland is an old one. Says he:

"Nothing can now be believed which is seen in a newspaper.
Truth itself becomes suspicious by being put in that polluted vehicle. The real extent of this misinformation is known only to

those who are in situations to confront facts within their knowledge with the lies of the day. I really look with commiseration
upon the great body of my fellow-citizens who, reading newspapers, live and die in the belief that they have known something of
what has been passing in their time; whereas the accounts they
have read in newspapers are just as true a history of any other
period of the world as of the present, except that the real names
of the day are affixed to their fables. I will add that the man who
never looks into a newspaper is better informed than he who reads
them, inasmuch as he who knows nothing is nearer the truth than
he whose mind is filled with falsehood and errors. He who reads
nothing will still learn the great facts, and the details are all false."

What Englishmen esteem as dignity is a quality
rarely found in American newspapers. Sensational
news-items have a prominence unknown in the average
English newspaper. Of course I except the *Pall Mall
Gazette,* which has discredited us in many ways. During General Grant's illness bulletins appeared by the
column twice a day. These columns were made up
of the most trivial matters. The *Post* one day announced that "at 6:35 a servant raised the blind and
opened the window to let in fresh air. Half an hour
later the window was closed and the blind lowered."
Even the best New York papers have a funny column
like the English country weekly; and in their items of
domestic news they compare with the *Penny Budget* or
the *Police News.* Murders, elopements, scandal of all
kinds, occupy the front pages of even the most reputable journals. In England we confine our scandal-mon-
gering to the doings of dukes, princes and lords—and
Heaven knows we have more than enough, even thus
limited; but in America, as the *Nation* complains, "nobody is too low to have his quarrels, sufferings or in-
trigues set forth at length; and the papers teem with
'spicy' reports of the elopements of bartenders and ser-

vant-girls, the scandals of unknown families, and the divorce suits of people whom nobody ever heard of."

The *New York Herald* in its Sunday edition of February 7, 1886, contained four columns cabled from Europe. Three columns of this was the description of a duel between two French journalists, and the other detailed the horrors of a French execution!

Of course there is a demand for this kind of reading. Servant-girls and labourers have money to spend on newspapers; and where these are conducted solely on business principles, that is money-making principles, editors must cater to all. Then there are hundreds of hysterical women-readers of whose tastes one knows nothing, until some interesting murderer like Guiteau or Maxwell has his cell piled up with letters and gifts of flowers and fruit. An anarchist condemned to death for murder is wooed and won by an heiress. In England if such a class of maniacs exists, it does not betray its presence by showering favours on murderers. The nearest resemblance I remember was that of the crowd of women who lavished dainties and flowers on Jumbo. And even about this there was probably a good deal of "Barnum."

A stranger sometimes has his attention caught by an attractive head-line, and beginning to read gets half-way down the column before he finds he is reading a quack advertisement. Readers who are used to journalistic tricks look first at the foot of the article. There is a story of a clergyman who was so used to scrutinize the last line of everything he read, that from sheer habit he glanced at the end of the Sunday morning's lesson before reading it in church.

If one were to judge by the newspapers, he would

conclude that the American people are the most un-
healthy in the world. Cures for the ills that flesh is
heir to, and many others that are acquired without
ancestral aid, are advertised in every sheet. America
appears to be the paradise of quacks. A character in
the old play *Nice Valor* says:

> " Never ill, man, until I hear of baseness;
> And then I sicken. "

The local politics of America probably keep the people in
ill-health.

Before I came to America a friend who had lived there
jocularly advised me to go into politics and get rich.
" But," said I, " one has to be a citizen to be able to
take office; and it takes five years to be naturalized."
" Then turn quack doctor for five years. That pays
nearly as well!" In bygone days a man who had failed
at everything else, bought a birch-rod and became
schoolmaster: in America he turns quack and the press
helps him to fame and fortune.

Early last year the *Tribune* appeared with a detailed
account of the excision by electricity of a tumour at the
back of the mouth. The next day it had nearly a
column under the following cheerful headings: " Ex-
ploring the Intestines: A Serious Wound skilfully
treated: A remarkable operation at Chambers St.
Hospital: The patient cured." This edifying article
began: " The abdominal cavity of man has always been
avoided by surgeons"—'and by writers in family newspapers,' might have been added. In such cases the
patient's name and address, age, occupation, are given,
together with particulars of his family, whether he or

any of his uncles and aunts have been divorced, imprisoned, elected to a public office, or suffered any other degradation, together with such additional details as may interest the cooks, chambermaids and male riff-raff who subscribe to the paper.

If, as it is said, there is always a soul of truth in things false, there must be a soul of truth in the American press. It is, however, unobtrusive, as is the nature of souls: it does not advertise itself in large caps, like the more carnal part of itself. For this reason it often remains concealed from those who do not know where to seek it. The original thought and writing found in American newspapers are of the highest order. The lack of protection to native authors forces men of the highest ability into journalism. With an international copyright law we might get more good books from America, but Americans at home would miss the clear thought and strong virility of style of many leader-writers. The Sunday newspapers abound with articles of great literary merit. Indeed they are more like our reviews than newspapers; but it is a poor compliment to the authors to mix such excellent work with scandalous personalities and blood-curdling crime-pictures. The *Tribune* has several very able writers on its staff; but their efforts are weakened by a puerile revision, which gives to every editorial the character of an indictment of the Cleveland administration. An article on the cultivation of sorghum may end with a lament that the business is unprofitable owing to the color of the democratic president's hair. The *Sun*, which aims at brevity, is a carefully written paper. Its financial articles are greatly esteemed. It is somewhat Anglopho-

bist. The *World* affords a wonderful example of what
energy and enterprise can do to make a paper successful. It built the pedestal to the Statue of Liberty,
and was in large measure instrumental in securing the
conviction of the dishonest board of aldermen in New
York. It has a well-managed detective bureau, and has
done much to ferret out criminals of all degrees. It is
sensational, which is one cause of its marvellous success;
but its boldness and persistency in attacking corruption
in high places more than compensate for this. At this
moment its big guns are directed against the corrupt
Commissioners of Castle Garden. The *Times* is among
the best of New York morning papers. It is well
edited, contains fewer horrors than usual, and its original articles are of the highest order. I may add that it
is a leading free-trade advocate. On this account the
judgment of an Englishman will be said by protectionists
to be biassed. The evening papers the *Post* and *Advertiser* rank very high. The *Advertiser's* business
columns are specially valuable; while the *Post* excels in
its leaders and leaderettes. The *Nation* I have put at
the head of the American press. It is a weekly publication devoted to the purification of politics and the
advancement of free-trade principles. Its original articles are thoughtful, independent and vigorous. It is
conducted in a dignified spirit; and its influence for
good is unimpaired by personalities and harmful news
items. The *Citizen* is a publication with the same aims.
The *Critic* is a weekly review devoted to literature and
art. It is ably conducted, and it includes in its list of
contributors the brightest names of American literature.
Comic papers are generally bright and clever, though
they seem to be at some disadvantage because every

newspaper has its column of fun, and even serious matters are often treated humorously. This is the way in which an editor announces the birth of a son:

"The angel of dawn laid at the threshold of Editor P. A. Barrett this morning a rosebud culled from the garden of the gods, as a reward for the energy and enterprise which have given Scranton a first-class daily. Mother and child are doing well."

Of bright, sparkling descriptions the American is a far better writer than the English reporter. In subediting too, in the display of news and its judicious distribution through the paper, I think the American excels. In the leaders there is little difference of merit. The Englishman is the more dignified, and his style is in keeping with the grave subjects usually treated editorially. The American likes " snap;" and this liking gives a precision and a crispness to his leaders, and a bright semi-humorous sparkle to his reports. It would be an improvement if some of the American brightness could be made to illumine our heavy verbatim reports at home. It would be like the bright crisp sunbeam of a winter's day falling athwart a London fog.

CHAPTER X.

ON THINGS IN GENERAL.

" Great Empire of the West,
The *dearest* and the best,
Made up of all the rest."

AB. COLES.

" WHICH of these roads leads to Skunk Hollow?" asked a pedestrian of a darky who stood at the junction of two mud-puddles. " Bot' on 'em, boss!" " And which is the best?" queried the traveller. " Dunno," replied the sable youth. " Why, don't you live about here?" " Ya-as." " Then how is it you don't know?" " 'Cos whichebber ob de roads you take, you'll be sorry you didn't take de udder one!"

And that is the kind of feeling the traveller has all over America. When Mr. Freeman visited Uncle Sam, he told him to mend his ways. But this would be a work of generations, and, with a ubiquitous railway system, almost a work of supererogation. An idea of the character of American country-roads may be had from the fact that it is not uncommon to go over them with a plough as a preparatory measure to repairing them, and sometimes the repairing gets no further.

Not only are the country-roads of America bad enough to justify the death penalty on a road-surveyor in England; but the pavements of cities are execrable. New York, which is by far the best taxed city in the world, has worse pavements than a German village. The road is full of inequalities in which the mud accumulates, to be splashed by horses and carriages over the clothes of pedestrians. Then crossings—there are no crossing-sweepers in America—are formed by huge monoliths, with large gaps worn between; and occasionally the unwary finds his foot slipping from the polished stone into eight inches of slush. The sidewalks are often raised a foot above the roadway, so that at every crossing one has to step that distance up and down, and a miscalculation of the height may result in a fall into the gutter. Further dangers await the pedestrian as he walks along. He presently stumbles over a portion of the pavement which is raised two or four inches above the rest, or kicks his pet corn against the raised covering of a trap-door. If it has been raining and freezing simultaneously, as often happens in winter, he may find his feet shoot suddenly skywards, and before he realizes the meaning of the movement, his head strikes an iron cellar door, which instead of being flush with the pavement is placed at a convenient angle for involuntary gymnastics. Undeterred by these diversions, the unsophisticated stranger proceeds, until his progress is arrested, say on Broadway, by the end of a cart which projects across the flags and occupies such portion of them as is not already covered by the boxes and bales which have just been taken from it. Silently rejoicing in the briskness of trade, he makes a détour into the muddy road and round the horses' heads, soon to be stopped again, this time by the scaffolding of a new building, which occupies the whole of the sidewalk. Possibly he here has the option of walking round the obstacle

Incident during a stroll.

by the road, or over it, by means of a wooden platform reached by five or six badly-built steps. If the pedestrian is a philosopher, and as good-tempered as all Americans are under small discomforts, he will cheerfully recognize in his walk an emblem of life with its perplexities and discomforts alternating with short periods of ease. He will also recognize and profit by the intellectual stimulus of such a walk: for one cannot surmount even trivial difficulties without the exercise of some ingenuity and intelligence. If, however, our traveller is an Englishman, with his ever-ready faculty of fault-finding, or an old gentleman with weak knees, or an old lady with poor eyesight, philosophy and good-nature will point to the ubiquitous tram-car. Taking perhaps the only vacant seat, our traveller soon finds that Americans are not deterred by considerations of personal or impersonal comfort from entering a car already full. If one hails a cab, he will probably be jolted stiff, and charged a dollar for a five-minute drive. Comfort in travelling in an American city is mainly a matter of chance. If few people are moving in the same direction, transport is rapid, cheap and comfortable. If one ventures into a street-car or on the elevated railway at the beginning or end of business hours, he finds a crowd of people wedged together on each seat, and a third crowd hanging on to the roof-straps, and convivially rubbing knees with those who are seated; but every individual amongst them as good-natured and contented as a boy on a toboggan-slide.

Many tram-cars in America are run without conductor. You place your five cents in a box with glass sides, near the driver. If you are a stranger to the custom and keep your nickel in your hand awaiting the collector, the driver fixes his American-eagle eye upon you, raps at the window, and tells you to "hurry up there." Everybody rides in street-cars. The pavements are too bad to walk on with comfort, and if they were better the American's time is worth more than the twopence-halfpenny charged for riding.

A common midnight apparition in Fifth Avenue is the machine street-sweeper. The scene in the moon-like brightness of the electric lamps is very weird. Pedestrians run into the nearest doorway, if a side street is not available. Then with artillery clatter come three or four machines, marching almost abreast. The dry dust rises in circling clouds above the horses' heads, remains suspended in mid-air until the sweepers are past, and falls again on the pavement like the gentle dew from heaven. The doorways then give up their living, who proceed along the silent streets, literally making tracks homewards.

Ash-barrels contribute much to the variety of a walk through an American city. These are placed in front of houses; and when the wind is not blowing, the stranger may amuse himself and add to his stock of knowledge by reading the queer advertisements that are pasted over them. If, however, a strong wind is blowing, literary diversions are out of the question, for one's eyes are busy shedding tears and washing out the dust which rises from every barrel like a pillar of cloud.

One of the numerous traditions that cluster round the memory of George Washington, is to the effect that he once threw a dollar from Mount Vernon across the Potomac; and another tradition which is acquiring the character of an historic truth, is that Senator Evarts remarked on this that "a dollar went further in those days than at present." Truly a dollar does not go far at present—not further than an English shilling, and not as far as an Italian franc. The poet who characterized Amer-

ica as the *dearest* land knew whereof he wrote. It is a land of inflated prices and artificial values. American productions are sold in England at half the price demanded in America. Among my papers I find the following extract from a newspaper, which well describes the facts in New York. I regret that I have neglected to notice the title of the book from which it is evidently a quotation:

"Incomes are large, expenditures keep pace, not on the old scale to which English society clings, but with a recklessness quite characteristic of the buoyancy of the American temperament.

Men seem to compete in expenditure as in trade, and New York has become the most expensive city in the world.

A modest house for a small family in a respectable locality cannot be had for less than £400 to £500. In the enormous 'flat' houses which are rapidly going up all over the upper part of the city, an apartment of seven or eight rooms, in nowise luxurious, costs £200 to £400 [say rather £400 to £1000], and in less eligible localities, and most moderate in pretension and accommodation, rarely less than £100.

At a well-known commercial restaurant a lunch off the joint, with a pint of cider and a cup of black coffee, costs 6*s.*, and is not nearly equal to the half-crown lunch of a London restaurant. The beef that is sent from here to England and sold at 6*d.* to 10*d.* a pound costs in New York twice that. The style of living which in London costs £1000 a year, here will cost £2000. The large profits are met by proportionate expenses. A man grows reckless of the dollars. At the hotels you not only pay enormous bills, but the greed of the attendants [who are rarely native Americans] makes it impossible to get decent service without continually tipping them, and not in the modest way one does in England. There is no charge made for service, but if you want your lunch served quickly and well you must fee the waiter when you give the order. He marks every *habitué;* who tips him and who does not; and the tips are on the American scale—anything less than a 'quarter' (a shilling) is contemptible, and the true American will never consent to be contemptible, even in the eyes of a waiter. He will at all costs avoid the reputation of meanness, and has little inclination to distinguish between meanness and economy, and, being always in a hurry to get back to business, says that he loses more than a shilling by the delay which the waiter imposes on him. At the hotel the guest who does not fee in advance soon finds the zeal of the waiters fall off.

You pay a boot-black a dime (5*d.*), and so on to the end of the list. And there are no suburbs to cheapen life. The Hudson River blocks one side with its uncertain winter navigation; and Brooklyn, across the East River, is as dear as New York (?), as a furnished flat of several moderate rooms there costs £25 a month. Everybody is so intent on his getting on that he does not stop to think that this system of enormous profits for everybody eats up

10

all his surplus gains; and a man who gets £500 a year here is no more comfortable than a London clerk at £250. There is the chance of a great hit, and he believes in his luck. The devotion to business is certainly phenomenal. If it is wise and healthful the future will tell better than to-day."

The difference in cost of living to workingmen, however, is not so great. I have obtained from a Scotch foreman in America a comparison of prices of food, clothing, fuel, and of rent, paid by workingmen in Pittsburgh and an ordinary Scotch town. This shows that in food the American workman has the advantage of 26 per cent, and in fuel 64 per cent. In rent the Scotchman has the advantage of 91 per cent, and in clothing 24 per cent. Altogether the Scotchman has a considerable gain. He gets for seventeen shillings and sixpence what the American buys for twenty-four shillings and tenpence.

The arrangements of a good American hotel or a first-class residence are far in advance of anything seen in the old world. Hot and cold water is found in every room, and often the electric light. Electric bells lead everywhere. Nearly all private householders have such electric communication with a telegraph office, that one ring will immediately bring an errand-boy, two a policeman, three an ambulance and doctor, four a fire-engine, and so on. All over the country private houses are furnished with telephones, and I have heard ladies say they would as soon be without a cook as without the telephone. In England the development of this system of communication has been hindered by the government, which had a monopoly of telegraphs, and it was held by the courts that the telephone was a telegraph. In this instance we have a clear proof of the injury which a government may cause by not minding its own business. In America private enterprise enables citizens to send money by telegraph and cable—a convenience denied to Englishmen at home. In some cities steam is supplied to houses, as gas and water are; and in Pittsburgh natural gas is furnished to householders *ad libitum* for what they previously paid for coal. At Lockport, power is supplied to factories by over-head cables at so much per horse-power. Speaking-tubes connect with the kitchen even in small houses; and a hoist brings up the dinner piping hot with no tumbling upstairs and smashing of dishes. Even in the "far west" these little aids to comfortable living are generally found; though one may there occasionally discover bits of Charles Dickens's America.

A newly-imported Scotchman, used to the simple fare of the Highlands, displayed great astonishment at the sight of an American table. "Look, Jock, mon!" he cried to a compatriot, "'taties for bre'kfast!" Sandy might have exclaimed at many other things on Uncle Sam's breakfast-table. According to Mulhall, our avuncular relative eats more than anybody else. He certainly cooks more, but he wastes so much that I fancy Mulhall's figures are misleading. Dr. Primrose said that the superfluous trappings of the rich were more than enough to clothe the poor. The waste of Uncle Sam would feed the hungry poor of any other nation.

The culinary art has attained a high development in America. Delmonico's has long held the palm against all Paris for good cooking; and the Hoffman House, noted from China to Peru as the most sumptuous restaurant and bar-room in the world, is now running its neighbour a hard race for precedence. Nature, having dealt lavishly with Uncle Sam in so many ways, has

The National Bird—with Cranberry Sauce.

capped her bounty by giving him the best food and the greatest variety of it. Indeed it is claimed that Chesapeake Bay is the gastronomic centre of the universe. Everything that can be grown in Europe, f r o m oranges to oats, Uncle Sam cultivates on his own farm, and it is as superior to foreign products as home-grown things proverbially are. In tropical Florida he raises tropical fruits. In Maine, in Wisconsin, he grows oats that make even Scotch mouths water. His Texas cattle now go to form much of the roast beef of Old England; and his Massachusetts cheeses are sold at the antipodes as Stilton, Cheddah, Roquefort or Gruyère, according to the taste of the purchaser. Salmon literally crowd his rivers, so that sometimes horses cannot ford them; and these he puts into cans and sends them by the ton to Europe, Asia, Africa; and his California peaches and apricots go with the salmon. American mutton is decidedly inferior to Scotch, Welsh, or even Australian; but that is a small drawback in the land of the terrapin, the canvas-back duck, that delectable anomaly the soft-shell crab, and the blue-point oyster. The annual production of the last-named succulent amounts to nearly twelve billion. New York alone consumes 810 million, an average of 660 per inhabitant. In winter, blue-points, invitingly lying on a sparkling bed of crushed ice, form the "grace before meat" at most American dinners. In summer, people ask a blessing by means of clams. I find that the prejudice against midsummer oysters is very old. Butler in *Dreyet's Dry Dinner,* dated 1599, says: "It is unseasonable and unwholesome, in all months that have not an *r* in their name, to eat an oyster." It is curious that clams are not eaten in England. They form a delicious appetizer before the soup; and clam chowder is a more epicurean dish than green turtle.

River and coast steamboats in America have been appropriately called floating palaces. In all kinds of unlikely places one finds rich woodwork, owing to the great variety and cheapness of timber; but in steamboats carpentry seems to have reached the dignity of a fine art. Then, in a clear bright climate where weather-changes are predicted with greater certainty than the rise and fall of stocks, there is no difficulty in keeping everything clean and bright. The difference between the dirty tug which takes passengers to their Cunarder at Liverpool and the beautiful steamer which used to transfer them to the Barge Office in New York, is as great and of the same character as that between a Galway peasant on his native heath and the statesman he becomes in America. A like difference is observed in the barges and other freight-boats of both countries. Those of England are black, dirty and often misshapen; those of America are bright, clean and usually as graceful as a private yacht. Charles Dickens's first impression of America was that everything had been newly washed. He was mistaken: it had never been allowed to get dirty.

The extensive use of anthracite coal keeps many American cities clean and free from smoke. In Wales there is an extensive bed of smokeless anthracite which would supply London for a century or more; but it would seem that the owners of the dirty, cheerful, bituminous coal have the market and are likely to keep it. Two and a half millions of people are clustered in and around New York; yet the air is as pure, and the skies as bright a blue, as in Italy. From the tops of the highest buildings, or from the great Statue of Liberty, one has a view of miles of buildings on one side, and a panorama of the beautiful harbour on the other, free from smoke and dirt. It is just the view to make the New Yorker glad, the Chicagoan envious, and the Briton proud; for was it not the last who first saw the capabilities of this beautiful site?

The love of the beautiful in nature is so recent an addition to the faculties of man that one may almost say it is a product of modern civilization. A primrose on a mossy bank was never anything more than a primrose until our grandfathers' day. Yet the products of past generations of men invariably appeal more to our æsthetic sense than do the works of the present age. Here is an anomaly. And again, how is it that the stolid Swiss, who remains unmoved amid his grandiose surroundings, evolved the graceful chalet, while the more highly-developed American never created anything finer than a log-house? The utilitarian spirit seems to have killed even the aspiration for the beautiful which generations ago had begun to manifest itself in New England. At Yonkers a man reputed to be worth sixty thousand dollars a year utilizes the lawn of his hired house for raising hay. And who has seen the glories of the Hudson without being shocked by the hideousness of such places as Peekskill? It is hardly an exaggeration to say that, out of the old settled districts, there is nothing rural in America. The country is unkempt. Snake-fences, rocks degraded by quack advertisements, unpainted wooden houses, garbage piles at the doors—such are the tokens of rural life in America. As a native has well phrased it, "there is a great deal of land, but very little country." And then the country railway stations! Who shall describe their unqualified hideousness, their chilling desolation, their unwelcoming emptiness? Often their ugliness has carefully been made worse. On the Erie Railway at a small station just outside Jersey City, an old locomotive tender has been deprived of its wheels and labelled with letters a foot long "Garbage Box."

Prof. Fiske, writing on the advantages of infancy, shows that the development of man to his highest form is dependent upon the training made possible by prolonged infancy, and that the false notions, superstitions and mistakes of the child are really useful elements in its growth to adult life. The same has been said of a nation. Indeed it is now a commonplace that societies are organisms, and subject like them to laws of growth and development. But America had no infancy. In three generations it sprang from the position of a province into the foremost rank of nations. Accordingly we find in American life an absence of what Carlyle called "the rich invigoration of crude beliefs and superstitions;" and the same great grumbler unwittingly excused many of the crudities he blamed when in his luminous language he said the American was "orphaned of the solemn inspiration of antiquity." The author of *The Biglow Papers* expresses in touching language the same thought:

" O strange New World, that yet wast never young,
 Whose youth from thee by gripin' want was wrung,
 Brown foundlin' o' the woods, whose baby bed
 Was prowled round by the Injun's cracklin' tread,
 An' who grew'st strong thru' shifts, an' wants an' pains,
 Nursed by stern men with empires in their brains!"

We often hear that Uncle Sam inherited from the old
nations much of his material greatness; but on the other
hand he seems to have lost by his deprivation of infancy
much of that vague quality which has been styled
"sweetness and light," and which includes a love of the
beautiful. America is but a vast workshop and kitchen-
garden. Its floor is littered with the *débris* of industrial activity. To complain of its unæsthetic character
is perhaps like grumbling because the floor of an iron-
foundry is not carpeted. A general sweeping and clean-
ing up would be premature, leading only to waste of
trouble, for the floor would soon be encumbered again.
There has been no time for this; but it is coming.
Already, the offices of Uncle Sam are models of comfort, and even of beauty. Perhaps his cities, streets
and country lanes will soon follow.

Between fifty and sixty years ago the Americans introduced into their country the locomotive. They had
been watching with interest the experiments of Stephen-
son in England, and no sooner was success achieved than
they adopted the crude idea and began to develop it.
It would be hard to say which nation has since made the
greater advance in railway construction and management. Both England and America have left the rest of
the world behind; how far behind one can only realize on
seeing some of the primitive " puffing billies" of France

and other Continental nations. But they have advanced along divergent lines; so that comparison is not easy. For comfort in travelling the palm must undoubtedly be awarded the nation that invented the sleeping- and drawing-room cars; and that at an early date ceased to build railway carriages after the design of the old stage-coach. Here, in an American's rejoinder to an English-man's unfavourable criticism of transatlantic methods, we have a terse description of the way Uncle Sam travels:

" We take first-class tickets that cost us $1\frac{1}{2}d$. (3 cents) a mile. A porter meets us at the entrance and takes our valise. We enter a car in which there are a number of comfortable arm-chairs. These chairs swing around, so that we can face the windows the passengers, or one another. If we wish to be exclusive we take a compartment—for two, four or six, as we please. But as I enjoy plenty of air I choose the main body of the car. At my elbow I find an electric bell, in answer to which comes a negro waiter who is ready to bring you anything—from a telegraph blank to a lunch. The floor is well carpeted and each chair has a big foot-stool. There is a smoking-room at one end of the car fitted up in leather, as well as the usual convenience of wash-basin, soap, towel, lavatory, etc. A little table can be fitted at your seat which can serve you as lunch- or card-table. The car stewards make tea, coffee and chocolate. On short distances many neighbors are apt to be on the same car, and a drawing-room is the best counterpart of it."

In England we are locked up in a narrow compart-ment with eight or nine other people, all wedged to-gether on two seats, and half of us with our backs to the engine. We have no arm-chairs, no waiters to bring us lunch, no lavatory accommodation—nothing in fact to relieve the tediousness of the journey or the discom-fort of our crowded position. If we get hungry, we run into the refreshment-room of some station for a sandwich, or buy a lunch-basket and use our knees for a table—the other passengers looking on with that British stolidity which foreigners so often mistake for something worse. As for lavatory accommodation on a train, the majority of the English people have never heard of such a thing! They are not supposed to require such accommodation while travelling—or if by chance they do, they wait till the train stops! We are a very long way behind America in comfortable travelling.

East of Chicago the speed of trains compares not unfavourably with that of the best trains in England. On short local lines, too, the comparison holds good; and the slow and wearisome trains of, say, the Lancashire & Yorkshire or the Southeastern have their parallels in America. Artemus Ward is accredited with a good story in this connection: When the conductor was punching his ticket—which he does about every tenth mile—Artemus remarked: " Does this railroad company allow passengers to give it advice if they do so in a respectful manner?" The conductor replied in gruff tones that he guessed so. " Well," Artemus went on, " it occurred to me that it would be well to detach the cow-catcher from the front of the engine and hitch it to the rear of the train. For you see we are not liable to overtake a cow, but what's to prevent a cow strolling into this car and biting a passenger?"

Passengers are in the habit of placing their railway tickets conspicuously on the front of their hats, so that the conductor may take and punch them to his heart's content without disturbance. I once saw the passengers in a West Shore train curiously classified by the conductor: those going beyond Albany had a plain red card thrust into the ribbon of their hats or pinned to their shawls, and those stopping at Albany were labelled with a white ticket. On some Western lines the conductor gives you in place of your coupon a coloured ticket, on which is printed your destination with a list of intervening stations and distances, and the direction, "Keep this ticket visible." You accordingly wear it in your hat, and the conductor knows where you are going at a glance. Americans are always amused on their first journey from Liverpool to London at our slow-and-easy ways. That the train should pull up just outside the station, while men go from carriage to carriage collecting tickets, is as great a surprise to them as the Continental conductor is to Englishmen when he clambers along the rushing train and suddenly appears at the window with a cry of *Billets, messieurs!*

The American system of checking luggage—or baggage, as Uncle Sam prefers to call it—is excellent. You tell the hotel clerk you are going to Kansas City on the eight o'clock train. Presently he gives you a number of brass checks, each representing a package, and tells you that your luggage has been taken to the station. At the station you walk to your seat in the train, which has been engaged by the same Genius of the Ring, the hotel clerk. In three or four days, as you are approaching Kansas City, a boy walks through the train jingling a number of brass checks on straps; and to him you entrust your checks and say where you want your luggage sent. Shortly after you get to the hotel, your trunks are brought upstairs, and then you see them for the first time since leaving New York. You have travelled fifteen hundred miles without a disquieting thought concerning the "impedimenta," as the Roman appropriately called his luggage. An American, habituated to this system and travelling in Europe, often thinks he has slipped back into Roman times. A story is told of an American travelling in England who required the guard's constant reassurance that his trunk was all right. At every station he put his head out of the window, and cried, " Conductor, is my trunk all right ?" " Yessir, it's in the back van," blandly replied the guard each time. But presently the guard grew tired of the ever-recurring question, and the answer "yessir" came shorter and took more the character of a hiss. " Is my trunk all right ?" asked the American for the thirteenth time. The guard drew himself up in front of the window, and fiercely regarding the anxious Yankee, replied, " If God had made you an elephant instead of an ass, you'd have been able to take care of your own trunk." With characteristic good-humour, the American told the story against himself.

Americans in England are always greatly entertained by our tavern signs. Our green dragons, blue lions, white harts, pig and whistles, cock and bottles, bull and mouths, are a source of constant interest and amusement to them. And of course they are less attentive to the entertaining signs and notices to be found all over their own country. Yet these are often more curious than the quasi-heraldic devices of our country inns. A notice in a New England card-room informs patrons that " The proprietor will do all the swearing, getting drunk, and vulgar talking for the establishment." In the Cambria County court-house at Ebensburg, Pennsylvania, a notice artistically displayed and printed in black and gold runs as follows : " If you expect to rate (expectorate) as a gentleman, you will use the spittoons and not the floor. You will also refrain from defacing this fine building in any way. Compliance with this gentle reminder may avert legal penalties." Here is another eloquent and firm admonition to good behaviour. It is in a printing-office in New York:

GENTLEMEN ARE POLITELY REQUESTED

NOT TO

YELL

IN THIS OFFICE.

I have heard of the following suggestive sign placed near the till in business houses:

"The Lord helps those that help themselves; but the Lord help those that help themselves here!"

In Broadway a tradesman's sign reads

JONAS BLANK PANTS EXCLUSIVELY.

This does not mean that Jonas suffers from chronic asthma: it means that he sells nothing but trowsers.

Under the Grand Union Hotel at Saratoga the sign of a "tonsorial parlor and capillary studio" reads thus: "Any colored hair bleached blond in an hour." At the Philadelphia swimming-bath a notice is displayed indicating the hours set apart for "Ladies and Misses," and "Gents and Masters." An "omnifarious store" is a common sight "out west;" and I have seen this all-inclusive sign supplemented by another: "Groceries, tripe, pigs' feet, saurkraut, hot coffee, birch beer;" and by the door were boots, tin pails, trowsers, a clock, goloshes, petroleum barrels, empty biscuit tins and a milk-can. The most startling sign I have ever seen is the one common on the rocks of Broadway, the fine road that runs along the Hudson from New York to Albany. It is terse and resonant. It seems that after some religious fanatic had painted on the rocks such exhortations as "You must repent or go to hell," some other lunatic erased the first four words, and the remainder is left to cheer the weary wayfarer as he trudges from New York.

The school-girl who figures in *English as she is Taught* was mistaken when she said "Climate lasts all the time, and weather only a few days." In America it is just the other way about. Indeed it is probably a mistake to talk about the American climate at all. One might as well speak of the stratum of the earth's crust. There are innumerable climates in America, and sometimes they are all operative at once. The people of California boast about the number of distinct climates found within the limits of their State. They need not. There are just as many to be found in any other State. In New York, for instance, they had 95° degrees one day, and a snow-storm the next. At Greeley, fifty miles north of Denver, the mercury dropped from 50° to 2° in little more than an hour. In Denver itself it fell thirty degrees in eight minutes. At Yuma in Southern California it is hot enough to give probability to the story of a soldier who, after dying there, found himself obliged to return to earth for his blanket. And it was not to heaven that he had gone!

In Minnesota they have one hundred and sixty climates, ranging anywhere from fifty-five degrees below zero to a hundred and five above. The trouble is that one never knows one day at which end of the barometer the climate is going to be the next day. It is interesting to watch it leap up and down the mercury-tube, but it is trying to the complexion.

There is one kind of American climate that is worthy of special notice. It comes in the late fall, in the winter and early spring. It fills people with electricity so that they are constantly going off in little explosions, and giving shocks instead of handshakes to their friends. When this particular dry, cold climate is operative, it is possible, after shuffling across a woollen carpet, to light the gas by touching the burner with the finger. There is a quick snap, a stinging shock, a little blue spark, and presto! the gas is alight. A newspaper—tissue paper or a silk handkerchief is better—briskly rubbed against a mirror, will adhere to it and crackle if torn away. I have had writing-paper cling to my hand, like tissue paper to amber, or stick to the window-curtains when thrown against them. This is a very wonderful kind of climate, and brings such a flow of spirits as to make one certain that Mr. Mallock never was in such a meteorological environment : else he would never have asked his lugubrious question. One Englishman who experienced the exhilaration of this climate exclaimed, "I see why you Americans do not drink champagne : you breathe it." But they drink champagne all the same !

CHAPTER XI.

THE PROFESSION OF POLITICS.   WITH A STORY OF A DOG.

"The Public!   Why, the Public's nothing better than a great baby!"—CHALMERS.

A S Colonel Ingersoll was one day standing on the deck of a steamer, he was accosted by a solemn-looking man, dressed in black and bearing other evidences of a religious profession. "Sir," said the divine, in a loud voice so as to attract the attention of other passengers, "I understand that if you had directed the Creation, you would have ordered things differently." The Colonel, after vainly trying to evade the man, was obliged to reply that he might have made some such remark. "Then," said the cleric with a smile at the on-lookers, "will you tell these friends in what particular you would have made things different?" "Certainly, sir ; I'd have made good health catching instead of disease." "Eh ?" ejaculated the astonished ecclesiastic. "And," continued Col. Ingersoll, "I would have visited on the third and fourth generations, the virtues of the mothers instead of the sins of the fathers !"

Robert Ingersoll is not the only man who would have ordered things differently at the Creation. Most people the world over would have left out lawyers. Uncle Sam would have stopped the creative process just before it reached professional politicians. Though other improvements would have been made or suggested by some of Uncle Sam's boys, yet in every part of the Republic unanimity would have prevailed in this matter of leaving the professional politician uncreated. If he, with his "boss," had had to spend eternity in excursions through space as a nebulous cloud or as a fortuitous cluster of soulless atoms, Uncle Sam would not have relented : he would probably but have coined another verb, and said, "Let them excurt !"

A member of this unnecessary profession, while criticising an opponent, has furnished an example of what is known in the American neology as a "complete give-away ;" that is, he inadvertently let us into the secret of his class. "Gentlemen," said he, "there is a theory, pretty well substantiated by facts, that a death and a birth always occur simultaneously, and that the spirit of the dead man enters the body of the new-born child. I have very carefully investigated the record of my opponent, and I find that when he was born nobody died."

A soul indeed would be but a cumbersome appendage to the professional politician. All that he wants is a slight foreign accent—a brogue is preferable—and a willingness to enter political life as soon as he gets his luggage—if he have any—through the custom-house.

11

Such a one, redolent of patriotism and whiskey, was accosted on his arrival at Castle Garden, and asked to which party he belonged.

"With grave
Aspect he rose, and in his rising
    seemed
A pillar of state; deep on his front
    engraven
Deliberation sat, and public care;
And princely counsel in his face
    yet shone,
Majestic though in ruin."

A pillar of state.

"Is it parthy ye mane?" said he ; "O'ch, Oi'm agin the gover'mint !" And so he was. So are they all, until they get into the gover'mint themselves. Even then they are not at rest. They remind one of their compatriots in our own council-chamber. They recall the countryman's description of his new dog. Said he: "The fust night I locked him in, and oh ! he jist howled and tore 'round that kitchen like all possessed, and in the mornin' I see he had gnawed a hole pretty near through the door, tryin' to get out. So I thought if he would ruther stay out than in, I was willin', and the next night I locked him out. And all night long that dog run 'round the house, and howled and whined and scratched and made a tarnal fuss, and in the mornin' I'm darned ef he hedn't gnawed a hole a'most through the door frum the outside, tryin' to git in, and I says to myself : 'You cussed fool ! wun't nuthin' satisfy you ?' So the third night I left the kitchen door wide open,

so's he could please himself 'bout stayin' in er stayin'
out, and dern me ef that dog didn't set right in the
doorway all night and howl about nuthin' !"

" Wun't nuthin' satisfy you ?"

Americans have been known to regret that they were
not born in Ireland, so that they might have something
to say about the management of their great land. But
the average native republican has no time for politics.
As Bill Nye says : " He seems to be so busy paying his
taxes all the time that he has very little time to mingle
in the giddy whirl of the alien. That is why," he adds,
"we are always in a hurry. That is the reason we have
to throw our meals into ourselves with a dull thud, and
hardly have time to maintain a warm personal friend-
ship with our families."

A negro was sauntering along the street with the
happy deliberateness of his race, when a policeman
brusquely shouted, " Get out of the way, you nigger: here

come the representatives."   " De representatibs ! who's dey ?"   " The Representatives of the People, you blun-

"I'se de people derselves!"

der-head !"   " Ump !" responded the darky with ineffable scorn ; " de representatibs ob de people ! *I'se de people derselves !*"

There is nothing so grave that it cannot be made to look funny if reflected by a convex mirror. Rousseau was present at the death-bed of a woman in whom the death-rattle was heard with the giggle excited by her own joke. There is an uncanny mingling of the death-rattle and giggle in American politics : a good deal of facial distortion to get fun out of solemnity. The only condemnation reserved for many kinds of wrong-doing in America is a laugh. The degradation of State and municipal politics is, for the most part, but a theme for the funny column of the newspaper. Men who fix their gaze intently on the clown's view of life, are apt to mistake the leer of a skull for a grin of merriment.

Censor of public morals.

Patriotism, which Dr. Johnson defined as "the last refuge of a scoundrel," is mainly a sentiment for banquet toasts and odes to the star-spangled banner. The ship of state is manned by a crew of self-seeking politicians, who see in patriotism their opportunity, and in Canada their refuge. So long as she keeps afloat, the owners of the ship are content to let her drift, while they devote themselves to paddling little cock-boats of their own. Only when the ship gets upon the rocks, as she did twenty-five years ago, are cock-boats and private life-buoys thrown aside. Then, indeed, the nation can rise as one man, with Spartan patriotism and Spartan heroism. Nothing so well indicates the strength of the federal system as that it should have survived disruption during half a century of political corruption. If the federal government had been corrupt—say as bad as the governments of States and large cities, it would perhaps not have survived disruption.

A Texan lawyer recently produced in a court of that State a petition addressed to the County Judge, signed by a large number of the most respectable and intelligent people of the place, asking that a leading and greatly esteemed citizen should be summarily hanged. *Not one of the signers knew what he was signing.* The petition was got up to illustrate the worthlessness of such documents. It also illustrates the off-hand way in which citizens perform such public duties as they undertake.

We are often called upon to admire institutions which invest every man with the rights and privileges of citizenship—the right to vote. We have imaginative pictures of

> " The freeman casting with unpurchased hand
> The vote that shakes the turrets of the land."

Yet we read in the New York *Independent* that nearly half a million registered voters in New York State neglected in 1880 to exercise their high prerogative. This means that one citizen in every three so little admired these institutions of equality, that he failed in his first duty of citizenship. First duty, did I say? There I am wrong ; for the first duty is to register, and here the failures cannot be counted. The small school-girl who recently defined the Constitution as " that part of the book at the end which nobody reads" wrote better than she knew. There are in the various New England States some legal antiquities called Blue Laws which are a good deal laughed at nowadays. One of these laws of Massachusetts reads : " It is ordered, that whosoever of the Freemen does not appear at elections in person or by proxy, he shall be for such neglect amerced to the treasury, ten shillings. " This law might do good if revived. The New American party in California demands some such compulsion. But to force a man by legal enactment to exercise a privilege is nearly as illogical as Carlyle's notion that men have a right to be forced to work.

New York has just learned an old truth in a new form; her board of aldermen, her " Collective Wisdom," her "government," is simply a band of rogues. The newspapers are full of righteous indignation ; and truths long suppressed or ignored are published in large capitals. Yet there is little excitement except among journalists and the gang itself. There is no popular demonstration, such as I read of at Salford, where a defrauding official has just been discovered. Let me quote a few paragraphs from the New York papers. With the present indrift of radical legislation to manhood suf-

frage and paid politicians in England, such lessons as
we can draw from the experience of America are especially valuable. We may also get a glimpse of the
working of the political machine, the Caucus, which
has been introduced among ourselves.

[*New York Times.*]

Dr. Crosby makes a certain broad analysis of the 250,000 voters
of the city. Of these he says 60,000 are made up of " the idle,
the ignorant, and the criminal," who cast their votes at the beck
of a " little knot of unprincipled idlers" into whose hands " our
want of care and watchfulness for our city has thrown the whole
management of its government." Thirty thousand more " who
could do much to offset this foul vote" do not take the trouble to
be registered and to vote. " They have no conscience regarding
their duty to the city that protects them and in which they pros-
per." The great bulk of the remaining 160,000 voters " humbly,
unresistingly follow the lead of the political party to which they
belong, which party is managed by the wretched stuff found in
the first 60,000." Perhaps out of the whole mass of 250,000, he
adds, " we may count 20,000 as casting independent votes for good
men and receiving the maledictions of the party organs for doing
so." . . .

The very condition of the public mind which has produced the
state of things under which good men groan, and against which
they protest, is the chief difficulty in the way of applying the obvious remedy. If these people of New York have not cared
enough about their public interests to guard against official incompetency, dishonesty and corruption, or to check it in its begin-
nings, will they exert themselves to eradicate it now? Are they
alive to the evils of the saloons which thrive by their patronage or
their tolerance, and do they care much to " squelch" the nuisance?
The primary evil exists, we fear, in a low standard of honor even
among the great mass of the most intelligent citizens, in a blunted
moral sense and indifference to abuses that should excite indignation, in the utter absence of a pervading public sentiment which
may be successfully wrought upon to bring about reform.

[*New York Advertiser.*]

This city is robbed, plundered, oppressed and atrociously mis-governed by its worst elements; thieves and "fences" and cor-rupt bargainers become city officers or city legislators; rascals with money buy from rascals in office whatever they want of privilege; and all because better men, led astray by political zeal, make bargains and "deals" and coalitions at election time.

[*New York Post.*]

There will be no surprise in this community to learn that one of our Aldermen was a regular receiver of stolen goods—an ac-complice, indeed, with a notorious band of thieves. What else can we expect when we choose our Aldermen from liquor stores and gambling dens? Jaehne was a silent partner in a liquor store before he went into the jewelry business. He is a fair sample of the morality of our average Aldermen. So long as we make the liquor business a training school for local statesmen, we must ex-pect to get this kind of Aldermen. The wonder of it is that we allow such a board to remain in existence. That we should not only allow it, but should actually put in their hands the power of selling for their own private advantage railway franchises worth millions of dollars, is not merely a wonder, but a disgrace.

Gotham is not the only misgoverned city in the United States. The *Advertiser* says:

New York only furnishes the most flagrant illustration of a sys-tem which has already become established in all of our large cities. The Boston *Record* has just done a good piece of journalistic work by looking up the occupations of all the members of the Demo-cratic ward and city committee, which dictates the Democratic nominations for city offices, which nominations are ratified at the polls. The committee consists of 279 members, and of the whole number seventy-eight, or considerably more than one quarter, are engaged in the liquor business, while fifty-eight are office-holders who secured their places through subserviency to this interest. Together these two classes constitute within four of a majority of the body, and as their personal interest in politics insures their attendance upon meetings in much larger proportion than other classes of the membership (among whom, by the way, are seventeen men whose names could not be found in the directory), it is obvious that they can control its action all the time. The impudence of the liquor element in Boston is shown by the fact that since a law was passed prohibiting the granting of licenses to saloons within 400 feet of a school-house, it has forced the abandonment of more than one school-house in order to prevent the closing of saloons in the neighborhood which were run by politicians."

The citizen who wants to control his own actions, and to have his country honestly governed, is in a strange dilemma. If he pays his legislators a salary, his council-chambers are soon overrun with unsuccessful business men, idle young lawyers, and half-educated failures of all descriptions, who cheat and pilfer him until he is distracted. If, on the other hand, he does not pay his legislators, he is overrun by men who have made a fortune in business and now enter politics to carry out some theory of government evolved in the counting-house; and by these his constitution is ever being patched up and tinkered, or his actions controlled, until he is swathed in red tape, like an Indian papoose. It is possible of course that the system of paying legislators would work better in England than it has worked in America, because with us the pursuit of wealth is not carried to so great an extreme. Perhaps our best men, men whose positions place them above a bribe, would still enter political life; but it is certain that the salary would attract many who are not so happily placed. And this would be a calamity we should not calmly invite. Honest men will soon quit a profession which entices rogues. The advocates of paid legislatures should examine the system in America before trying to establish it among ourselves.

The professional politician here described is not the one who occupies the presidential chair or sits in the senate. Things are not so bad as that. Despite the insinuation of a prominent English journalist, "If by a surprise of fortune, the President happens to be a gentleman," the First Magistrate of the Republic is generally a man of honor and education; while not a few have belonged to that class of nature's noblemen who rank above "gentlemen." The professional politician here meant is the City Alderman or State Representative, but more frequently the political boss—the man who creates the President and makes senators. Every important official is nominated in a convention of politicians, who are usually without office themselves, and his name is placed by them on the voting ticket used by electors at the ballot. Though any elector may make out his own ticket, and vote for himself as mayor of his own city, he knows full well that no candidate stands the least chance of election unless nominated in the usual way and joined to the party ticket.

Raw material.

Hence electors, rather than throw their votes away, prefer to choose the least objectionable of the nominees of the bummers, as these caucus-leaders are named, but as the proverb has it, "there's little choice in rotten apples." These are the men who really make the government. Their power, however, is on the wane, especially in federal politics; but in the governments of States and cities they have a power almost incredible.

I can name several cities where as many as forty thousand votes have been controlled by men with such names as Jerry Mulroy, Barney Biglin, Buck Brady, John Kelly, Boss McLaughlin and Johnny O'Brien.

Finished product.

But even the great federal Congress which is sometimes held up as a pattern for us to copy, is hardly worthy the encomiums which have been so freely lavished upon it. A body of men who are so blind to the necessities of their native literature, and so oblivious of the just claims of foreign writers, as to refuse an international copyright law, barely command our respect, much less veneration. A Collective Wisdom that mistakes what is gainful to a few capitalists for what is profitable to a whole nation, does not appeal with overpowering eloquence to our admiration. Then what shall be said of its recent pension bill? There was hardly a newspaper in the country, republican or democrat, that did not support the President's veto of this pernicious measure, which was passed in the House by a vote of 180 to 76, and in the Senate without a roll-call. Amid such a chorus of approval as followed the President's act, one was fain to ask, " Whom and what does Congress represent ?" and to sympathize with the answer, as given in *The Epoch* : " Certainly not the public sentiment which finds expression in the majority of reputable newspapers, and evidently not the sound commonsense of the American people, which has been appealed to with apparent effect by the President's veto message." The fact is that Congress, recently called the " most august body in the world," finds itself ungracefully sticking on the horns of a dilemma. The tariff system has called into existence interests which are powerful enough to make or unmake any party. On the other hand, the revenue accruing to government vastly exceeds its legitimate expenditure. To curtail the income they must meddle with the tariff ; but that would not be tolerated by the protectionist party. So nothing remains but to increase the expenditure—somehow. A pension bill including in its benign operations even deserters and rogues, is one way out of the difficulty. Another is the building of a navy, which under the control of some " Jingo" statesman of the future, or in command of some enterprising admiral, may lead the Republic into a war which will effectually remove the difficulty of the surplus. In this way there may be reached an equilibrium, which, however, will not be rest.

It must not be supposed that the American's apathy to politics is never thrown off. A stranger arriving in the midst of a presidential campaign, would think that every citizen and candidate for citizenship had gone wild on the subject of politics. Electors and non-electors parade the streets in their thousands, night after night, grotesquely garbed and carrying torches, marching in military step along the uneven and often muddy pavement, cheering, yelling, singing. Rockets shoot across the sky with hoarse shrieks, or lodge in some chimney-stack, unpleasantly suggesting the snort of the fire-engine, which sometimes comes in as a sequel to these demonstrations. I have seen a torchlight procession of this character eight miles long.

Then who shall describe the intense interest of the party "managers" when their candidate is nominated? Who shall tell of the quiet dignity of the nominating convention, the sachem-like gravity of its members, and the silent solemnity with which its decision is received? Here is the choice finale of a four-column description of Mr. Blaine's nomination, in the *Herald,* June 7, 1884:

"Then pandemonium had its own. Barnum's stuffed eagles, owls, 'My Country, 'Tis of Thee,' cheers, shouts, 'Yankee Doodle,' rebel yells, cornets, drums, hats, canes, 'See the Conquering Hero Comes,' umbrellas, sheaves of wheat, the infernal din of Henderson's gavel, the deep booms of outside cannon, responded to by the hurrahs on the inside—a half-hour of utter confusion and incessant uproar—that's what happened, occurred and proceeded."

After nomination, the candidate becomes public property. Every paragraphist has the right to recall everything that the aspirant for public honour has done and left undone; and to render it spicy and palatable to the public maw by condiments of exaggeration, scandal, lies and bad jokes. Mr. Blaine in his eloquent eulogy of President Garfield speaks of the "five full months of vituperation—a prolonged agony of trial to a sensitive man, a constant and cruel draft upon the powers of moral endurance" which follow nomination to the presidency. The American litany ought to be made to meet exigencies of public life by an additional clause: From public fame and defame, from scoffers, paragraphists and liars generally, Good Lord deliver us.

After election come other kinds of torture. In the Metropolitan Museum at New York there is a plaster cast of Lincoln's hand. Near it is a notice drawing attention to the fact that the thumb is swollen " from congratulatory handshaking"! This handshaking ceremony has to be gone through at frequent public receptions, when thousands of citizens step in and, ranging themselves in a long row, pass before the Chief Magistrate to shake hands with him. Then so "cabined, cribbed, confined" is the presidential office, that Mr. Cleveland, soon after his election, found it needful to deny a rumour that he had been fishing on Sunday, which in some States is a punishable offence.

Then come applications for office as thick as locusts. Some of these get into the papers, or are concocted in the newspaper office. The *Arkansaw Traveller* is authority for the following caustic letter to the President from the late postmaster at May Bloom, Arkansas:

"I don't kere nothin' for the money that's in this office. A dollar an' a half a year ain't no more to me than 75 cents is to you, but I don't want to be fooled with. Shortly airter you tuck your seat a man wanted to bet me that you wouldn't be in office mor'n a year till you would make some big mistake. I bet him a cow. Airter I got your notice tellin' me to git out, I driv the cow over to the feller's house, an' told him he had won her. You not only cut a man's pride, but you break him up in bus'ness. I believe you take pleasure in makin' a feller feel bad, an' I don't believe you're much uv a Democrat nohow."

The subscription recently started for a monument to General Grant recalls a similar subscription raised twenty years ago. Some twenty thousand dollars were collected soon after Lincoln's death for a monument to him. The sum was invested in government bonds and placed in the Treasury. In March, 1885, the *Tribune* announced that there remained but fifteen hundred dollars of it; the rest had been spent in salaries and designs for the monument. The monument itself *had never been begun!*

Does this disorder imply a failure of republican institutions ? By no means. The government of America was manufactured. It did not grow as governments normally grow. The period of the Revolution was one of active political speculation. Rousseau had just formulated his ideal society founded on the equal rights of individuals; and the world was everywhere busy with similar problems. The leaders of the Revolution were prepared by the thought of the day to recognize the republican form as the ideal government; and the peculiar inter-relation of the colonies made a federal republic the only form of union possible. Still, it was an ideal form, and required for its harmonious working an ideal humanity. The ideal humanity has of course been wanting; and that is why the federal republic has taken a form which was not contemplated at the outset. In other words, as men could not be moulded into harmony with their perfect institutions, the institutions had to adapt themselves to the imperfect natures of men. The political structure raised by Washington and the great men who surrounded him was a marvellous piece of architecture ; but its designers never dreamed that millions of aliens would crowd its halls and corridors, ousting and crushing the native American to the wall. When the constitution was framed, contingencies were undreamt of which have since become dominant political factors. The founders of the Republic, though they builded better than they knew, never contemplated the boss system, under which voters are led by thousands to the poll, there to vote as directed. They never dreamed of dangers to liberty arising from the German vote, the Irish vote, the liquor vote, a Senate of millionaires, or the evil influence of millions of illiterate aliens. But grave as these dangers seem, and baneful as is their outcome, one is reassured by the confidence of the Americans themselves. It is easy to mistake for a mountain the black cloud of corruption that overhangs the Republic as if threatening liberty with ruin and death; but the real mountain, concealed by the cloud, is the character of the American people—cold, impassive, but affluent in strength. The epidemic of dollar-hunting will not last forever. Men are gradually learning that money is not an end: that it is but an aid to the purchase of satisfactions; and they will presently realize that a pure government, a high standard of public life, an honest, unselfish public spirit, give to society a moral tone more satisfying to its members than anything that can be purchased by dollars, be they never so abundant.

CHAPTER XII.

RECIPROCITY IN CRIMINALS.

" One of the Seven was won't to say: that Laws were like cob-
webs, where the small flies were caught, and the great ones break
through."—BACON.

A MARYLAND divine
was passing through
the streets of Balti-
more one Sunday
morning a few months
ago, when his atten-
tion was attracted by
a group of boys play-
ing baseball. Accost-
ing them, he asked
why they were not at
Sunday-school. "The
superintendent has
gone to Canada, sir."
"Canada?" he repeated with a puzzled look. "Yes,
sir; he was a bank manager." The minister resumed
his walk with saddened mien as he thought, "Nineteen
centuries of Christianity have not made men honest."

Defaulting bank managers who are also Sunday-school
superintendents are not peculiar to America: they have
been heard of in pious Scotland. What is peculiar to
America is the premium put upon peculation by public
12

indifference, and by the facility with which legal punishment may be avoided. The journey from New York to Montreal is to an American hardly greater than the run from London to Brighton to an Englishman. Imagine the demoralization which would result if London thieves of all grades, from pickpockets to absconding cashiers, were guaranteed immunity from punishment by a little trip to the seaside. That is exactly the condition of affairs in America. Thieves and other criminals who love not "the gladsome light of jurisprudence" find a safe haven and congenial fellowship in Canada; and in Montreal there is fast forming a social set of ultra-exclusiveness, composed of every type of unconvicted criminal. Extradition treaties are like Bacon's cobweb, allowing the great flies to break through. Every legal manœuvre has been tried to secure the punishment of the rogues who are living at Montreal in luxury on the proceeds of their villany; but countermeasures have always balked justice, and hordes of thieves and swindlers are still at large.

Whenever a criminal of greater audacity than usual crosses the frontier with his carpet-bag well lined with plunder, the republican press sends up a wail of indignation and despair. The Canadian authorities are denounced for the legal laxity that promotes such dishonesty in a neighbouring state. This is doubtless a right view to take; but in the absence of voluntary aid by Canada, ought not the federal government to try to secure some remedy itself? Untrammelled by red-tapeism, men outside the sacred temple of the government think they see an easy remedy. Uncle Sam pleading with Canada for the criminals she is sheltering beneath the union jack, does not present a dignified figure; nor does Canada appear to greater advantage. It is curious that in matters which are outside the province of government, people have great faith in its efficacy, and constantly appeal to it; but here, in a case where govern-

ment alone can do anything, people content themselves with reproaching the colonists, and leave the real remedy untried.

I emphasize the fact that Canada offers a ready asylum to criminals from the United States, because a great many people in England regard the Republic as mainly the producer of dynamiters and the protector of English thieves and forgers. It is well to know that there is complete reciprocity in criminals between Britain and America.

One of the most difficult problems that await the coming American is the reconciliation of religion and morality, or, in default of this, the construction of a code of practical ethics, capable of standing without the prop of a religious sanction, and fitted to modern society. Supernatural religion has lost its hold on the minds of a large and increasing class of people. This is admitted even by the religionists, who often speak of the atheistic tendencies of the age. Supernaturalism is giving way to Rationalism. In America, the process has advanced a long way—even further than in Germany, for there the movement, though general among the cultured, does not extend to the mass of the people as it does in America. The writings of Spencer, Darwin, Huxley, Tyndall, Fiske, Wallace, Haeckel, and the lesser prophets of the new faith, are in the homes and minds of the people. They are working important changes in men's estimate of life and its purposes—changes which are not always beneficial to the individual affected. Religion and morality have been made so interdependent by ecclesiastics in the past, that many people think they are identical; and when such people throw their religion overboard, their morality generally goes with it. It is not the new faith that should be blamed for this: it is the old one, which taught, not that morality was a good thing in itself, but that the goodness lay in obeying a commandment. Most men now realize that there are crimes undreamt of by Moses, and unnamed in the Decalogue, more heinous than that of coveting a neighbour's ass. The American morality, not yet evolved in its completeness, will probably teach in simple phraseology that "it pays to be good, therefore be good" !

The age we live in is responsible for many forms of crime unknown to previous ages.

The Irish-American dynamiter, for instance, who periodically frightens the women and children of England by breaking windows and getting himself sentenced to penal servitude for life, is a product of nineteenth-century civilization equally with the penny post, railways and a free press. These are the days when the impurities of the social organism are working out, often by means of open sores. The corruption of centuries of class-government has come to a head; and we are witnessing changes akin to those wrought out by the French Revolution. It is indeed but a sort of French revolution, adapted to our own age, and modified by small doses of constitutionalism. We may not realize it, but the age we live in is fraught with peril to creeds substantial as well as to "creeds outworn." Movements are now being set up which will roll on into distant ages. Political methods, social forms, religious beliefs —all are being attacked, and some will surely go down before the onslaught. And the base of operations against European systems is often in America. There the descendants of Russian serfs, Scotch crofters, Polish refugees, evicted Irish peasants, deserting German conscripts, and other victims of old-world tyranny, are living and working for their own good and no longer for the aggrandizement of superposed classes. They are doing more. They are carrying an active propaganda into their own country—amongst their old friends and relatives who still suffer under unequal laws in opprobrious poverty —for in Europe poverty is opprobrious. These are the

men in whom ages of repression are bursting into a reaction which threatens ruin to all government, good and
bad.   It is not in America that

> " vows to break the tyrant's yoke
> Expire in Bacchanalian song and smoke."

The power and extent of the dynamite conspiracy, however, are overrated by Englishmen.   Americans recognize in Rossa a mere windbag, who gets the contribu-
tions of unthinking Irishmen and servant-girls by blus-
ter, and spends them on the same—himself, namely.
They laugh at the tirades of the British press whenever
a dynamite explosion breaks a window or throws down
a fence.   Rossa, who is reputed to be of mild dis-
position and is celebrated by comic journals for his

charity, is really but an impudent
fraud.   The majority of his kin in
America disown him; and some of
the strongest denunciations of his
policy have come from Irishmen.
When Mrs. Dudley shot him in
New York, a great laugh crossed
the face of the Republic.   He did
not then pose as a martyr, but as a buffoon.   Here
is an example of the ridicule in which Uncle Sam indulged:

> " Oh, I am a bloody old dynamitard !
>   Sing biff ! bing ! fizzety-bang !
> The hand grenade and the big petard
>   I'm fixing to fling in the queen's front yard;
> Sing ho to the lad from Skibberdedang
>   Who'll demolish the queen's dominions!

Nitro-glycerine is my daily drink!
 Sing smash! crash! lickety-slash!
And the daintiest food is powder, I think;
 I can chew up a cartridge without a wink,
Blue vitriol I use to season my hash,
 For my appetite's like my opinions.

Ah, here comes a girl with a little gun;
 Sing help! murder! call the police!
Whatever I've done was always in fun,
 And rather than fight I'd always run.
Sing ho to the lovely paths of peace,
 And blest be the queen and her minions."

It is a mistake to suppose that the Irish in America are all worthless as citizens of the Republic, or Fenians in their relation to England. With their patriotism for Ireland there generally lurks an affection for the great Empire of which their own little Emerald is but a part: a part, though, that has contributed far beyond its proportion to make the Empire great. Not only has Ireland given us Wellingtons and Wolseleys; she has always furnished the stalwart backbone of the rank and file of our army.

Individually, the Irishman is the most generous, lovable, hot-blooded good-for-nothing. Full of brightness and mirth, a hospitality that inquires not the nationality of the recipient, and a love of kin and the "ould counthry" that nothing can quench, ages of misgovernment have not marred him beyond recovery. Here is testimony to his credit: The remittances by Irish settlers in the United States to friends in Ireland between 1851 and 1887 amounted to twenty-four and a half million sterling. In 1881 more than a million and a half sterling was thus sent—an average of nearly

five shillings to every man, woman and child in Ireland !

More than fifty years ago the following protest against
pauper and criminal immigration appeared in the *New
England Magazine* (vii. p. 499 [1834]):

"The drones that 'Europe breeds in her decay' are shaken
from her lap upon the blooming bosom of our own delightful
land. The sluices of a polluted emigration from the old world
are freely opened to us, and the defecated dregs of centuries are
drained off. Heaven knows that we would not exclude from the
blessings of our free government, and our generous soil, the honest and the industrious of other climes, simply because they may
be poor or unfortunate. We would fling wide our portals, and
bid them enter. It is a proud title for a country, that of the
Asylum of the Oppressed. As Americans we glory in it. But we
do most decidedly protest against having the nation converted
into one vast lazar-house, for the reception of the sturdy beggars,
the contented paupers, and all the *mauvais sujets* of England and
Ireland, who may be shifted upon us by fat capitalists, better able
than we to bear the incumbrance. Unless the evil be checked, it
will distend itself until it press like a horrid incubus upon the
energies of our high-minded native population."

England and Ireland have not been the only offenders.
I once read in an old American newspaper that an Aus-
trian ship of war had just arrived, and in an imposing
manner landed a cargo of paupers and criminals at New
York! Perhaps it is these "dregs of the effete monarchies" who are now returning to Canada and Europe
as defaulting bank presidents, Polish anarchists, Russian conspirators, and Irish dynamiters. If so, here is
poetic justice ! At any rate, it is certain that American
prisons and workhouses are largely filled by foreigners.
The census of 1880 showed that, while the foreign-born

were only thirteen per cent of the entire population, they furnished nineteen per cent of the convicts in penitentiaries, and forty-three per cent of the inmates of workhouses and houses of correction. The immigrant seems to control the liquor traffic of America. In 1880, of the traders and dealers in liquors and wines sixty-three per cent were foreign-born, and of the brewers and maltsters seventy-five per cent, while a large proportion of the remainder were of foreign parentage. Of saloon-keepers about sixty per cent were foreign-born, while many of the remaining forty per cent were of foreign extraction.

The anarchists who so often enliven the public prints by what reporters love to call "Communistic blood and thunder" are mostly foreigners. America is not only the paradise to which the shades of dead socialists go; it is also the happy hunting-ground of living communists. It is they who are at the bottom of the troubles that so often set capital and labor in antagonism. At Detroit Polish strikers were amenable only to the exhortations of their native priest. In the Connellsville coke regions Hungarian labor-troubles were unmanageable because the rioters did not understand English. The Chicago anarchists who threw the bomb among the policemen were foreigners with only one exception; and at a socialists' meeting in New York at which the wife of one of the condemned anarchists spoke, the audience did not understand enough English to take off their hats in presence of a lady as she bade them. Foreigners form the nuclei of the secret societies which exist in every American town. Chicago alone is said to contain more than twenty thousand men pledged to the destruction of "monopolies," which in the socialists' vocabulary means the destruction of society.

Herr Most, who was imprisoned in England for incendiary writing in the *Freiheit*, is a conspicuous character among transatlantic socialists. Not long ago there was a free fight at a socialists' meeting in New York, and Most received a good drubbing from some left wing of his party. This fanatical German has given a definition of a revolutionist, which is instructive reading:

"The revolutionist," says he, "has no personal interests, concerns, feelings or inclinations; no property, not even a name. In the depths of his nature, in words and deeds alike, he has fully broken with the civil order, with customs, morals and usages. He is the irreconcilable enemy of the world; and if he continues to live, it is only to destroy it with the greater certainty."

There is a thoroughness about this which is truly admirable. There is no hair-splitting here, no half-spoken theories, no equivocal metaphors or algebraic signs. When we get a statement like this, we know exactly what we are dealing with. And its horrible candor is not made more comforting when we hear from Prof. Mezzeroff, of the International Dynamiters College, that he will continue to teach the manufacture of the deadliest explosives "until every workingman in Europe and America knows how to use them against autocratic government and grasping monopolies." This gentle Russian says:

"I have the receipt for forty-two explosives in a burglar-proof safe, and if I should die, they will be published to the world in order that all may know how to deliver themselves from tyrants and those who wrong them. I can take tea and similar articles of food from the family table and make explosives with them more powerful than Italian gunpowder, the strongest gunpowder there is."

And with a bland simplicity that is almost endearing, he issues the following invitation to the free-born citizens of the Republic.

"If we want to kill each other, let us do it on business principles. Gunpowder kills at the rate of 1,200 miles a minute, dynamite at 200,000. If you use my explosive you can defend yourself against the armies of the world."

One sometimes hears that these men are gentle and kind to their families: that they love the prattle of children; and that they often display a benevolence that belies their professed hatred of society. It may be true. They certainly display a bland innocence in their published writings. To think that society, emerging from barbarism after untold struggles towards the light, can be thrown back into chaos by a small group of half-educated, half-sane theorists, is childlike indeed. I do not share the apprehensions of some writers, who see nothing but evil ahead. We should welcome these theorists as tending to good rather than harm. Their wild utterances often indicate real grievances; and amid their ravings one may occasionally hear a new argument. But there is no real danger. It is contrary to the nature of things that increasing knowledge should tend to the disintegration of human society. The progress of knowledge is indissolubly bound up with the progress of mankind. Socialism, anarchy, and all the other ulcers which are spotting the body politic are unquestionable indications of ill-health; but they are not proofs of a moribund condition. That these extreme ideas prevail is a proof that the present industrial and political systems are not in harmony with the human nature living under them. Until harmony is reached—until equilibrium is estab-

lished, there will continue this and similar forms of
motion among the parts.

But even the optimist must admit that an oversight
is being made in educational methods. While we are
surrounded by new conditions, education continues in
its ancient rut. Boys and girls in every city and ham-
let are wasting precious hours conjugating verbs and
making declensions, while their fathers in the workshop
are listening to the revolutionary theories of German
and Russian exiles, whose notions of society are utterly
incongruous in a republic. It is of ever-growing importance that education should fortify the mind against
those crude theories of society which have been fostered
in the malarias of European despotism.

But Uncle Sam gets better stuff from Europe than
the paupers, criminals and anarchists complained of.
He annually gets hundreds of thousands of brawny immigrants who become honest and thriftful citizens, and
who, entering his workshops or settling on the western
lands, are aiding in the formation of the greatest nation
the world has yet seen. Of the 169,000 cotton opera-
tives enumerated in the census, only 94,000 are native
Americans. In the woollen industry the foreign workers
number 35,000 to 53,000 natives; in iron-works the
proportion is 52,000 foreigners to 72,000 natives; in
glass-works, 7000 foreigners to 13,000 natives; in
carpet-mills, 8000 foreigners to 9000 natives; in screw-
works, 460 foreigners to 990 natives.*

---

* These are " protected " industries, and the foreign element
is thus seen to have a disproportionate share in the alleged bene-
fits of the tariff.

The immigrants who landed in the United States in the year 1882 numbered 788,992; and in the five years ending 1884 the number exceeded three millions. And there are millions more waiting to come. Bismarck says the German people have now but one desire—money enough to carry them to America. It has been estimated that the cost of rearing and educating a man is £300. Accepting this valuation, and also the estimate of the immigration commissioners that each immigrant brings into the country an average of £20, we find that Uncle Sam has here a source of wealth richer than the mines of Golconda or Peru. During the last six years he has received from Europe a free gift valued at six thousand million dollars ! Surely this will content him! It is a magnificent set-off to the few hundred good-for-nothings who have been foisted upon him.

CHAPTER XIII.

UNCLE SAM'S SUPERIORITY.

" I earn that I get, get that I wear; owe no man hate; envy
no man's happiness; glad of other men's good."—*As You Like It.*

THE title of this chapter recalls a story of
Sam Echols, traditions of whom still lin-
ger around his native city, Atlanta. Sam
was endowed with great ability, but his
towering self-conceit exceeded all his
other natural gifts. His opinion of himself may be dimly comprehended when
stated in his own words. One day, when he was reading law, he laid his book aside, and turning to a fellow-
student said: " When I think of the strength and wide
range of my mental faculties, and the variety and extent of my attainments, I stand back and look upon
myself in utter amazement. So far as I can see, I am
complete. I can think of nothing that is wanting. I
would not give a snap of my finger to add to my present
stock of knowledge one more fact or one more accomplishment!" When rebuked for his overweening vanity,
Sam calmly replied that he was not conceited; he was
simply conscious of his own phenomenal powers and
acquirements. Our avuncular relative is similarly un-
conscious of self-conceit; but he is equally sure of his
own greatness.

I have frequently asked Americans in what particular they considered their country in advance of the rest of the world. Invariably the first and only indication, named in an off-hand way, has been "Yankee inventiveness." Lately there have been several attempts to identify national greatness with statistics of bacon and flour-barrels. "Republican institutions" is often assigned by those who forget that Rome, with its ignorance of personal rights, was a republic. France, too, with her conscriptions and meddling wars with savages, is a republic, though imperialism is dominant in all her institutions. And was it not in the American Republic that slavery longest survived among civilized nations? Not republican institutions, therefore; though it would be bad for America to be without them. The federal system of government is without doubt the source and promise of all true greatness in America. It is difficult for Europeans to realize this. Indeed few Americans fully appreciate its importance. To them it is very like the law of gravitation, ever operative, rarely felt. The federal principle is a political law of gravitation, keeping forty-seven units in mutual contact and interdependence. An illustration may help to a conception of its importance.

Imagine all the states of Europe, from Turkey to Denmark, united under a common government, appointed by manhood suffrage among the people of every nation. Imagine further an independence of these nations in respect of internal affairs, as complete as that they now enjoy. Such are the United States of America. Forty-seven States and Territories, so large that the average is more than twice the size of Portugal, existing in peaceful union and unanimity of feeling on federal matters,

while each in regard to its own affairs is as independent
as Sweden is of Spain—this is surely the most wonderful political aggregation the world has ever seen.

Within these forty-seven States and Territories there
exists perfect freedom of trade. Over distances exceed-
ing that from Europe through Central Asia to India, the
products of any State are transported without inspection
or tariff. Varying in their soil and climate as greatly
as any portion of Europe differs from the rest, these
States have all the advantages that would accrue to the
old world if all fiscal barriers were swept away, along
with the remnants of feudalism maintained by them.
The internal commerce of America has called into existence 135,000 miles of railway to supplement its vast
river-ways and lake communications. The amount of
merchandise passed annually over these railways, freshwater seas and rivers, dwarfs into insignificance the sixteen million tons of exchanges which foreign ships effect
between America and the old world. The freight annually carried by rail alone exceeds three hundred million
tons; and the gross earnings of the railway companies
amount to one hundred and sixty million sterling. Fully
seventy-five per cent of this merchandise is for home
consumption. Then besides this enormous railway
transportation, coast and river steamers move more than
double the tonnage of foreign exchanges.

Commerce is the simple exchange of commodities, and
so long as these get into the hands of the consumer it
matters little whether they come from Tartary, Tim-
buctoo or Maine. It is rather the quantity and quality
of an article, and not the place of its growth or manufacture, that most concern the person using it; and
that American consumers have quantity is shown by

the fact that the internal commerce of the United States divided amongst the population averages seven tons per head, against six tons in Britain, although a greater proportion of the latter is for export. The merchandise sent from New York to San Francisco is, so far as distance can make it foreign, as foreign as that sent from Liverpool to Philadelphia; and exchanges between Baltimore and Chicago have as foreign a character as those between London and Genoa. America presents, indeed, the greatest example of free trade the world has ever seen. It is also the most beneficent; for without this free trade there could be no Union. In presence of this achievement, it is not difficult to believe that Tennyson's ideal may be realized, and that we shall yet attain to the "Parliament of man, the Federation of the world"! If there be perfection in political institutions, it is the federal system. Who can limit the capabilities of man under such a system—especially if it become universal? What increased happiness to humanity, what a cessation from drudgery, what a glorious ending to class-hatred, would result if by some magician's wand Europe could be federalized on the American plan, and men's natures simultaneously made fit for the change! That were a Utopia indeed!

The workers of Europe, besides maintaining prolific royalties, aristocracies, and numerous parasites whose sole functions are sleep, digestion and procreation, also maintain in unproductive labour several millions of soldiers. Add to this incalculable tax, the cost of preparation for war, and payments on war debts, and we have a faint idea of the burdens under which European industry competes with that of America, whose army is one tenth smaller than that of the toy-kingdom of Roumania!

13

The struggle for existence has begun afresh. This time it is a struggle between large civilized nations, not small hordes of savages. Not brutal strength is here the test, but ingenuity, intellect, and economical methods and institutions. It is a simple question of arithmetic as to which will survive, unless the policies of the warlike nations of Europe undergo a change. The struggle is industrial, not military; and the serried ranks of European bayonets and Krupp guns will avail as little against an industrial war as they would against hunger or disease.

This Confederation of Peace is the great sign-manual of America's superiority. Her ingenuity in potato-peeling machines and the like is as unimportant in this light as are the antiquated and useless sword-buttons on the lappet of a philosopher's coat, considered as adjuncts to his intellectuality. In presence of this great verity, which gives to Uncle Sam's face the glow of Sinai, dudes, Anglomaniacs, trivial signs of social atavism, journalistic eccentricities, all sink into insignificance. As Lowell sings:

> " These are the mountain-summits for our bards,
>   Which stretch far upward into heaven itself,
>   And give such wide spread and exulting view
>   Of hope, and faith, and onward destiny
>   That shrunk Parnassus to a molehill dwindles."

The great fact stands prominently forth like America's colossus of Liberty enlightening the world, that the peoples of many states, united in bonds of peace, are working together for the elevation of man into something better than a butcher of his fellows, something nobler than the cringeing subject of a king, something

greater than the feeding-machine of aristocratic idlers—
A MAN! Well may humanitarians throw up their hats
and cry *Vive la République!*

But all this in the present year of grace is excessively
Utopian. We Englishmen have yet to acquire the right
to live undisturbed by neighbours, before we can disband
our armies, scuttle our navies, and settle down to the
propagation of Quaker tenets and free-trade principles.
So long as our next-door neighbour carries a revolver in
his belt with the avowed intention of shooting us the
first time he finds us unarmed, we should be foolhardy
to go abroad with nothing more formidable than a Bible
precept or a quotation from Longfellow. I am proud to
believe that the earth would not have been half so de-
sirable a place to live upon, but for England's contribu-
tions to our comfort; and I further believe that if England were blotted out of existence to-morrow, the world
of the future would be much the worse for it. On
purely humanitarian principles, therefore, it is permis-
sible to advocate the preservation of our beloved little
island. Let us be sure, therefore, that our navy continue
the best, and our army the bravest; and let us resist the
tendency which prevails among some very good people,
to trot the British lion around
in a lamb's skin. The much-
derided song that gave the
Jingo party its name ex-
presses a sentiment that most
Britons feel. "We *don't*
want to fight;" but we should be unwise to allow the
rest of the rhyme to lose its truthfulness.

It is a worthy thing to have high motives; and I am

glad that our army and navy have such a plausible justification as that of the future welfare of mankind. But behind the humanitarian is the Englishman, who, if other reasons fail, would see England exist for her own dear sake. After living in many lands, I know that I have a warm corner of my heart kept sacred to the universal brotherhood of man; but the heart itself is English to the core, and never yet failed to give a little flutter at the sight of a union-jack.

We ourselves are talking a great deal of federation nowadays—federation of that mighty empire which covers a fifth part of the globe, of which the mother-country is but one-seventieth portion, and which is at least three times larger than the great land of Uncle Sam. Sixty-five territories and islands in every part of the globe, containing an aggregate of nine million square miles, and over three hundred million inhabitants—such is the British empire, in which that of Rome in her palmiest days would be but a province. To form a confederation of this! 'twere a consummation devoutly to be wished. There are objectors in plenty. Let them enumerate the difficulties to be overcome. For my part, I admire the intrepid spirit and broad views of the promoters, and wish them Godspeed! Already among the English-speaking peoples of the world there is a federation of thought and sentiment, an alliance of mutual appreciation, and a community of good-will that are ever binding the parts together perhaps more firmly than legislative bonds could do. As Senator Evarts says: "Nothing is provincial any more and nothing central. English people are everywhere surrounding the world with their speech, their laws, their literature, their affections. Wherever a man speaks English to English hearers, he is and speaks at home."

CHAPTER XIV.

UNCLE SAM'S WEAKNESS.

" No great genius was ever without some mixture of madness."
ARISTOTLE.

HILE in the South in the early summer of this year, I saw a group of negro boys engaged in a suggestive sport. They had caught a bullfrog, and had fastened fireflies all over him. The frog, not understanding the new lights that were breaking upon him, hopped about in utter frenzy; and the more wildly he jumped the greater was the delight of his tormentors. Many of Uncle Sam's boys are at present fastening fireflies to the bullfrog Protection, and great are its shifts to escape the illuminations put upon it. Let us join the sport for a few minutes. It is capital fun to watch the huge reptile dance around as the fireflies shed a gentle radiance over his back, revealing that this at least is not the toad that wears a precious jewel in its head.

To say anything against protection at this time of day will seem to many like slaying the dead lion. But the lion is not dead : he is only old and feeble. So let us trot him out, and try to hit him in a new place. Even if we don't hurt him badly, we can amuse ourselves by tweaking his tail as some western senators are fond of doing with that of the British lion.

If we adopt the American workman's estimate of himself, we shall have to qualify the ideas we have got of his ability from abstracts of Uncle Sam's balance-sheet lately published. Instead of being the energetic, active workman we have pictured him, he is a poor listless fellow, who is devoid of energy and lacks the enterprise and skill of even the "pauper labourer" of Europe. Thus recast in the native mould, our ideas of the American workman are vastly different from what they were. Let us look for a moment at this native estimate which is to effect such a modification of our own.

The natural wealth of America has already been spoken of in these pages. Its thousands of miles of coal, its mountains of iron-ore, its masses of pure copper, and mammoth veins of gold and silver, its rivers of oil and wells of natural gas—all these have been mentioned with some envy, as have also the fertile lands which yield corn in an abundance that justifies its use as fuel. What an industrial paradise is Pennsylvania! Coal, worth sixteen shillings a ton in England, I have seen used as ballast for railroads or thrown into heaps as worthless. The deepest mine in the coke region is only three hundred feet deep; while the surface of the land yields forty bushels of wheat to the acre. Coke of the best quality sells for less than six shillings a ton. Coal is barely worth transportation—except away from the gas belt. At Lebanon, near Harrisburg, there is a mountain of iron-ore which requires no mining. Cars are run to the side of the mountain and the ore is shov-

elled in. Similar mountains are being discovered at
the head of Lake Superior. Gas-wells dot the country
in such profusion that half the gas is allowed to run to
waste, or is consumed in the profitless illumination of
the night. Oil flows in streams from scores of wells in
the same district.

Now look at Europe. England is the leading manufacturing country. Much of her ore is brought from
Spain ; her cotton comes from America, Egypt or
India ; nearly two thirds of her wool consumption—one
fourth the clip of the world—is imported from Australia
and South Africa. Of gold and silver she has none ;
of copper little in comparison with America. Her coal
is brought up from as great a depth as 2500 feet, and
is twelve times as costly as that which served Pittsburgh
as fuel before the discovery of natural gas. She has
no rock-oil, no natural gas. To these natural disadvantages are added the artificial burdens of army and
navy and the ever-growing royalties and aristocracies.
The British workman is not only disadvantaged in his
material conditions, but also by his feudal limitations.
Since 1850, dukes, marquises, earls and their relatives
and friends are estimated to have taken over a hundred
million sterling from the earnings of the working men
of England. The labourer's thrift is their profusion.
Taught by his church catechism from the earliest age
" to order himself lowly and reverently to all his bet-
ters ; and to do his duty in that state of life to which it
shall please God to call him," the British workman
rarely displays that enterprise and energy, that seeking
after new and better methods, which are connoted by
the phrase " independence of character," and which
are among the most admirable traits of the American.

In the rest of Europe industry is even more cramped and injured. Everywhere the man whom Americans call " the pauper labourer," works with artificial disadvantages superposed on natural ones. When with great effort he has delved into the earth for ore and brought it to the surface in scanty quantities, some prince or lordly parasite pounces upon his gains like an eagle on the booty of the fish-hawk. After he has converted the residue into iron, another pounce is made, and his labour is seized, perhaps to fashion a musket or a sword. Finally the labourer himself is pitchforked into a livery, forced to take the musket and kill other working men at command. Stated baldly, these are the industrial conditions of America and Europe contrasted. If, as the American workman contends, protection is absolutely necessary to his survival in this kind of a contest, in Heaven's name let him perish as a lazy shiftless fellow, who only encumbers the earth and ought to give place to any who can do better, be he heathen Chinee or "nigger"!

As a matter of fact, however, the American workman is neither lazy nor shiftless. His energy and enterprise are unlimited. He is a sober and steady workman. Mr. Pullman, who has dealt with hundreds of thousands of workers in his time, says he does not remember to have ever seen a native American workman in a state of intoxication. Another large employer with whom I am acquainted adds similar testimony. With these qualities the American workman joins an independent spirit which, once infused into the democracies of Europe, would promptly ring the knell of royal dynasties and aristocracies. I have heard it said that the American workman asks for bread, with a cigar in his mouth. Possibly he does; I never heard one ask for bread, though I can testify to the cigar : it is not a good one. But his manliness is such that no royal or aristocratic idler would be allowed to feed at the expense of his starving family.

Why then is there any need for protection ? There is no need for it. One reason why the protectionists are so strong in America is because so many people are incapable of comprehending large truths. The ability to form large conceptions of space does not necessarily include the power of apprehending great truths. The fallacy associated with the balance of trade is far beyond the comprehension of millions of people at the present day. It is only a hundred years since this fallacy was universally held to be a self-evident truth. Relatively to economic science, the majority of mankind are still in the middle ages. Another reason is that while the agricultural interests are dispersed over the continent, manufacturing interests are concentrated in rings, combinations and political clubs. Few wheat-growers of Minnesota recognize any community of interest with the tobacco-planters and cotton-growers of the South ; but the iron-manufacturers are wise enough to recognize a menace to their own monopoly in an attack on the cotton or woollen industry.

An old Scotchwoman was once taken by her husband to see the wonders of the microscope. When she saw animalculæ monsters engaged in deadly combat with each other, she arose in great trepidation and cried, "Come awa', John !" "Sit still, woman, and see the show," said John. "See the show, mon ! What wud come o' us if the awfu' like things should brak out o' the water ?" Uncle Sam looking at free-trade monsters through a microscope, occasionally starts back affrighted, and exclaims with pallid face, " What would come o' us if the awfu' like pauper labourer should brak loose upon us ?"

If any one wants to know the exact quality of the intelligence arrayed on the protectionist's side, he should write to the American Iron and Steel Association, Philadelphia, for their pamphlet of stories illustrating the evils that will befall the Republic if the pauper labourer of Europe is turned loose upon the defenceless American workman. I have not kept the title of the publication, but Mr. Swank will remember it from my description.

An American once remarked to me as I watched the customs-inspector turn over the contents of my portmanteau, " Our great nation doesn't show to advantage when it's mussing [i.e., making a mess of] a man's shirtfronts." " That's nothing," I replied, with some show of Yankee indifference ; " last Christmas some friends in Germany sent me a little book as Weihnachtsgruss ; it was stopped in the post-office, opened, assessed at a dollar and a half, and taxed ; and I received a notice as ' importer of books' to call personally and pay thirty-five cents. So I had to go down-town specially to get that book, climb up to the fourth story of the post-office, apply for the book, sign for it, and pay for it. Then your great nation gave me my property." My friend then told a story which was published in the *New York Times* of a German immigrant who landed in 1885 with a coat which he had bought in 1879. He afterwards lent the coat to his brother for use on a voyage to Europe ; and when he applied to the United States Treasury to be allowed to receive back his coat without paying duty, the government officials decided that, while the law allowed a man to wear the coat across the boundary of the United States, it could not be admitted free if sent by itself. So the garment was appraised, taxed fifty per cent on its value, and after infinite trouble and the payment of numerous charges, fees and dues, the German reacquired his coat.

I was afterwards witness of a worse example of governmental interference with private rights. At Venice last summer I accompanied an American lady to a furniture shop to buy a large tapestried chair. I bargained and paid for it. It cost three hundred francs; and this amount appeared on the receipted bill. The chair was consigned to an agent in New York; and the receipted bill was likewise sent to him. While the owner of the chair was still in Europe, the custom-house appraiser had the presumption to raise the valuation of the chair to 350 francs, and to add a penalty of sixteen dollars for wilful misstatement of its value! Vainly was it pointed out by the agent that the receipt corresponded with the shipper's invoice. The chair was taxed on the increased amount, and a further sum of sixteen dollars exacted as penalty. When the owner returned to America, she demanded restitution of the unjust fine; and received a reply from the Collector of Customs that, as the application had not been made within the period prescribed by law, there was no remedy!

At the time of the Revolution we read that the Americans were a nation of smugglers, and John Hancock was a chief of smugglers. History repeats itself. Few Americans to-day visit Europe without returning well laden with dutiable articles. On the hottest August days one may see ladies land in seal-skins, and men in top-coats, new clothes, and with their pockets full of gloves. And why should we blame them? The whole tariff system is a swindle; and citizens landing with their pockets full of European purchases are only evading what the common-sense of every one tells him is a swindle. If anything can justify evasion of the law, it is surely the degrading shifts adopted by Congress to get rid of the surplus without touching the tariff. The tariff makes prices so high, that it is a common saying in America that one can save the cost of the passage to and from Europe by buying a few suits of clothes or a Redfern gown while there. And not only do they save on cost: the clothes in Europe are of better quality. There is a duty of forty-six per cent on raw wool. The clip of the United States reaches three hundred and twenty million pounds, but the people could consume double that quantity. The result is that much cotton is mixed with the wool, and the resulting cloth is of inferior quality.

I have heard it said that free-traders have all the arguments, and protectionists most of the facts. Yes; but what sort of facts? Here is a protectionist fact, vouched for by no less an authority than Mr. Rowland Hazard of Rhode Island: In the United States from 1867 to 1877, while the duty on wool was at its maximum (45 to 55 per cent), the number of sheep fell from 39,385,386 [Mulhall says 42,300,000] to 35,804,-200. During the next four years, 1877–81, under a lower tariff the number rose to 45,016,224. And for whom was this industry "protected"? The mass of the poor who paid an augmented price for their clothes? By no means. The persons benefited were the rich squatters of the West who own vast flocks of sheep. A single squatter at Albuquerque, New Mexico, had 500,000 sheep—one seventieth of the whole! Protection, is it? Well may the American poet exclaim :

> " Let us speak plain : there is more force in names
> Than most men dream of ; and a lie may keep
> Its throne a whole age longer, if it skulk
> Behind the form of some fair seeming name."

One may say of the protectionist's " fact" as a friend of mine says of a lawyer, that it is like an old gun, apt to go off at the wrong end. In the same parlance, we may add that protection itself has a strong recoil; and hurts the shoulder of him who fires it. Here is one way in which the recoil hurts Uncle Sam: American exports to Europe, consisting mainly of breadstuffs, cotton and beef, have to pay an augmented freight often amounting to a hundred per cent, because ships must return to America either wholly or partially in ballast. Unless, therefore, an article will bear an artificially raised rate of carriage, it cannot be exported. The cost of navigating an empty or only partially-laden ship across the Atlantic is the amount of what is really an export duty paid by every cargo of American produce sent to Europe. It is also the amount of what is practically a bounty paid by Europe to India, Egypt and Australia on cotton, wheat and beef exported by them—a bounty which is rapidly raising up strong rivals to Uncle Sam in the provision markets of Europe. Can this be a factor in the decrease of cotton exports from 250 million dollars to 214 million during the last five years; of the decrease of exports of breadstuffs from 260 million to 125 million; of the decrease of exports of meat and provisions from 130 million to 90 million in the same period? The total exports of agricultural products have fallen from 730 million dollars in 1881 to 484 million dollars in 1886. This, meseems, is a rather hurtful recoil; and it strikes the most numerous of Uncle Sam's workers—the agriculturists, who are really three to one compared with the manufacturers. And while the exports of agricultural produce, thus reduced, amount to between four and five hundred million dollars a year, there is not a manufactured article except uncoloured cotton cloths (nine million), oil-cake (seven million) and refined sugar (eleven million) exported to the amount of five million dollars! These are facts—protectionist facts!

Only one workman in twenty, or five per cent of the labouring population of the United States, is engaged in protected industries; yet, according to Sir Lyon Playfair, in the last twenty-one years the people of America have paid two hundred and forty million sterling in the extra prices of home products. That two hundred and forty millionaire manufacturers have been produced is a questionable gain to the mass of the people.

A comparison has been made in this chapter between the conditions under which industry in Europe is competing with industry in America. With this comparison in mind, let us look at another fact or two. The protection accorded to the cotton-manufacturer amounts to over forty per cent; yet, the pauper labourer contrives to send back to the land of cotton-plantations and the birth-place of the cotton-gin thirty million dollars' worth of cotton manufactures per annum. In spite of the duty of thirty-five per cent, iron and steel manufactures to the amount of thirty-four million dollars are every year sent across the Atlantic to the land of iron mountains and natural gas. Silk manufactures protected by an ad valorem duty of nearly fifty per cent cannot compete with Europe; and nearly thirty million dollars' worth are imported. Sugar pays seventy-three per cent; and yet the amount imported is enough to give to every man, woman and child in the Republic about forty-three pounds of foreign sugar every year. And what about the woollen industry, which is protected by a duty of sixty per cent? No less than forty-five million dollars' worth of wool and woollen goods are imported every year. Plate glass paying the outrageous duty of 148.80 per cent is imported to the amount of half a million dollars a year! How are these for protectionist's facts—especially when taken in connection with that other fact that, with only two or three exceptions, not an American manufacture is exported to the value of a million sterling!

All this seems very anomalous, but it is easily explained. Let the explanation be in the words of Mr. Joseph Chamberlain, M.P., who, during his business career, was a manufacturer of screws. As reported in the London *Standard*, Mr. Chamberlain said:

" At that time the Americans put a duty of 100 per cent on screws, and in spite of that his firm sent these articles to America in large quantities. The result was that the American manufacturers came over here and said: ' We are making 100 per cent on capital; if you continue to send screws to America we shall, of course, be obliged to reduce our prices. That will shut you out, but it will reduce our profits, which will not be good for either of us. Let us, therefore, make a bargain; we will pay you so much a year to sit still and not send a screw to America.' Well, they did it, and his firm received a handsome income for years from the American manufacturers, protected, as they were, by the folly and stupidity of protectionist legislation, to sit still, and not send screws to America."

The last census stated that the screw-makers of the United States numbered 1361; of these, only 990 were native Americans. Admitting all that protectionists claim, it seems a high price that is paid for the "protection" of these 990 men. *A barbe de fol on apprend à raser !*

Facts! why, facts bristle all around us. They start up like the followers of Roderick Dhu from every bush and stone. The protectionist who calls for facts is like Cadmus sowing his dragon's teeth; but the crop of armed men is doubly and trebly iron-clad, so that they cannot even destroy themselves.

Here is a fact for the protectionists at home: wages in free-trade England are from thirty to sixty per cent higher than in protected France and Germany; yet English manufactures in immense quantities go all over these countries.

The periodical depressions and the panics which are so destructive of credit in America are mainly due to protection. An unnatural competition is set up amongst manufacturers which results in great over-production. Then come failures, and large stocks of goods are forced on the markets, reducing prices and causing more failures. Production then stops for a time, the public meanwhile getting cheap supplies and absorbing the surplus. The small capitalists having been ruined and forced out of competition, all goes well again for a time. There comes a "boom;" capital circulates, competition grows active; and soon the usual results of over-production ensue. And so in unvarying round—boom, depression, panic; panic, depression, boom.

There is an amazing amount of buncombe talked by politicians on this subject. In the presidential campaign of 1884 the Republican party tried to make the tariff question the issue of the contest; and it was asserted that the ever-increasing agitation for tariff reform had been brought about by English emissaries. This indeed became one of the rallying cries; and in the Republican processions banners announced that "British gold won't wash in this crowd"! The democrats were forced to try to checkmate the movement, and for a time their paraders marched in time to the cry, "No—no—no free trade!" It is always a safe piece of buncombe for a political candidate to denounce "British emissaries" who come to advocate free trade and the ruin of the helpless American workman!

It has been said that England ought not to complain: for America buys more of her than of any other nation. Granted: but she does not buy of us for love! If she could get what she wanted in other markets, she would do so. But here arises the inevitable *tu quoque.* England buys of America more than double what she sells to her: she buys 350 million dollars' worth, while France and Germany combined only buy 100 million dollars' worth. Indeed England is a better customer of Uncle Sam—I might say Farmer Sam—than the rest of the world put together. And be it remarked, in answer to our alleged ingratitude, that England is the only great nation from whom Uncle Sam does not buy more than he sells. If he were to "reciprocate" with us as he does with France or Germany, instead of buying 154 million dollars' worth of our products as he now does, he would have to buy from 400 millions to 450 millions' worth. Of course he buys from our colonies and India; but

14

he manages to sell enough to them to make a fair balance.

"What things are dutiable?" I heard a European passenger ask as he made the usual declaration before the customs officer. "Everything," was the reply. And "that is so." From his cradle to his grave the American is paying duties. As a baby he is swathed in taxed muslin. His little nose is wiped with a taxed handkerchief. His porridge is made from corn grown

under the stimulus of taxed fertilizers, and he eats it with a taxed spoon out of a taxed feeding-cup. The wheels of his baby-carriage are tired with hoops that have paid a duty of 2½ cents a pound. When he escapes from the taxed apron-string of his nurse, and finds shelter in the tax-supported school, his boots, his satchel, his clothes, his books, have all contributed their quota to the embarrassing surplus, or else helped to build up some mammoth fortune for a protected capitalist. The buttons on his trowsers and the bristles in his tooth-brush can be found in the tariff list. He is lulled to sleep with opiates that have paid a dollar a pound; and wakened by clocks that tick to the tune of twenty-five and thirty per cent. His toys are placed under an embargo of thirty-five per cent, and the firecracker with which he celebrates the Glorious Fourth costs him one hundred per cent beyond its value. The plums and prunes in his pudding have paid one per cent a pound to the Treasury; and if he is luxurious enough for raisins he pays two cents a pound. If he has a taste for shelled almonds he must pay seven and a half cents a pound duty, though—subtle discrimination worthy of legislators!—he may buy *unshelled* almonds by paying only five cents for the privilege. As he merges into adolescence, the American pays twenty-five per cent tax on his jewellery and fifty per cent on his gloves. The letter-paper and the lace handkerchief which he sends to his lady-love bear a similar relation to the national exchequer. His tobacco is taxed, and even free soap is denied him. Well may his hair turn gray before he is thirty! Well may he be gaunt and careworn, giving outsiders the idea that he has not enough to eat!

Of course under such a system of government coddling on the one hand and government interference on the other, there is nothing incongruous in a petition like the following from an "infant industry." According to the Leavenworth (Kansas) *Standard* it was sent by the bootblacks of Leavenworth to the Mayor and Council:

"We, the undersigned bootblacks, who by our industry support ourselves and contribute to the support of the families of our parents, respectfully request your honorable body to levy a license tax on bootblacks of $2 per annum, thusly protecting us in our endeavors to obtain an honest living, and stop the encroachment of the Chinese bootblacks, who are reducing the price below five cents a shine. We believe that the imposition of this tax exemplifies the principles of protection to American industry. It would protect us in our honest labor. Your favorable consideration of our position would forever tie us to a government of the people."

The last sentence has an ironical ring. The sight of a crowd of "protected" bootblacks tied to the government — to the grandmotherly apron-string, so to speak — would be an inspiring sight to a patriot of the political-boss stamp. And the *queue* might acquire that element of variety which always lends a grace to the picturesque, if the apron-string were passed on to the washerwomen who protested to the President against the Treasury towels being sent to the Chinese laundry!

A century ago the commerce of the world seemed to be passing under the star-spangled banner. In twenty years American shipping increased fivefold; and by 1820 "the Yankee clippers" had gained such reputation that Grantham says people used to go to Liverpool to see them. In 1826, when the decadence began, 92·5 per cent of the foreign carrying trade of the United States was done by American vessels. Yet in sixty years, by the operation of laws fitted to the time of Henry the Eighth, "we have reduced ourselves," says Mr. Edward Atkinson, "from the position of a dreaded maritime people to a position of comparative insignificance upon the sea. At the end of a century of vigorous life and effort we remain but a province, unable to keep our own flag at the mast-head of any fleet of modern vessels."

Only thirty years ago three fourths of the carrying trade of America was on native bottom. Now little more than one seventh is so carried. Of the nine and a quarter million tons increase in the American foreign trade, Great Britain has managed to secure nearly six million tons. Of every eleven steam-vessels carrying grain from New York in 1883, seven displayed the Union Jack, but none the Stars and Stripes. Of every eighty-three sailing-vessels laden with grain which left the same harbour, only one was American. In 1856 the tonnage of American vessels entered from foreign ports constituted 75 per cent of the total tonnage. In 1868 it had fallen to 35 per cent; in 1882 to 15·5 per cent, and it remains this year about the same! Yet we read in *Niles' Register* for 1830: "No interest in the United States has been so severely protected as the shipping. The 'American system' fully commenced with it in 1789, by *discriminatory duties* on imports and tonnage. On a vessel of 200 tons, laden with 150 hhds. of sugar, for example, the *protection* amounted to more than seven hundred dollars, enough to pay the *whole wages* incident to a West India voyage!"

These are protectionist facts, not free-trade arguments. To protect the iron, timber and other interests, the tariff raised the price of all ship-building material. Then, to foster a native seafaring population, other restrictive acts were passed, obliging American ship-owners to engage crews in America, where labour is thirty to fifty per cent dearer than in Europe. Thus the prime cost of a ship was artificially raised; then the cost of navigating it was unnaturally increased. Such a ship, of course, could not compete with those of England, which cost only half as much to build and navigate;

and the last American line of steamers to Europe passed under the Union Jack about two years ago. So died the American foreign carrying trade !

Despite all this muddle, the result of government meddle, we occasionally hear a heart-rending appeal to the Political Fetish for relief. It is almost incredible that in presence of these destructive effects of governmental interference with commerce, men still bow down before their Juggernaut! Here is an example from a newspaper:

"Shall England build our vessels and carry our commerce while our business languishes, our mines are darkened, our furnaces are cold, our mills idle and our workmen crying for bread? No, no! Let us make our own iron and steel, build and man our own ships, and strive to regain a commanding position in the ocean commerce of the world, for soon the United States will be able to export iron and steel to all the nations of the earth. Then we shall need a national merchant-marine to float our metals to the ocean markets of the world. Let the people cry from Maine to the Golden Gate for this national industrial necessity—the improvement of our merchant-marine by the help of the government."

Why, the government has been helping it all the time —has helped it out of existence! Truly, compared with this Political Superstition, the Voodooism of Southern negroes is positive philosophy, and the credulity of a Neapolitan woman godlike reason.

CHAPTER XV.

STAR-SPANGLED BRITONS—AND SOME OTHERS.

" For he himself has said it,
And it's greatly to his credit
That he is an Englishman!"

Modern Classic.

HE Englishman
abroad is prover-
bially a grumbler.
Even at home fault-
finding is his habitual humour.   Petty annoyances
which other people are
prone to 'pass over in silence, incite him to anger
and letters to the press.
Americans gauge everything by the question, " Does
it pay?" and rarely think it worth the worry and vexa-
tion to resist trifling aggressions.   Thus Englishmen in
America do not show to advantage.   They have more to
grumble about than at home; and they exercise their
prerogative regardless of the bad impression which
their avowed discontent may make.   To this hypercriti-
cal attitude must be ascribed much of that discour-
tesy which Americans think of as British ingratitude.
Everywhere in the United States one hears of English-

men who, while enjoying the hospitality of the country, did nothing but complain. Perhaps the offender supplemented his ill-grace by publishing the adverse opinions formed during a brief visit, emphasizing the things which displeased him, while lacking in due appreciation of the good things he found. I have before me the published comments of "a disillusioned Britisher," who spent a few weeks in what he calls a corner of the country. He travelled from Montreal to Baltimore! An American who had the temerity to pen an ill-natured attack on the British Empire after journeying from London to Canterbury would be rightly written down an ass, even by his own countrymen. This disillusioned Britisher betrays his animus when he tells us that for a whole hour he travelled watch in hand, counting the times the door of the railway-car was left open. And would you believe it, he got up to shut the door *one hundred and twenty-six times* in the hour—more than twice a minute! Heroic Briton! What sufferings were thine! And the glory of it! But is this the stuff that makes our race great, or is it that which makes our greatness little? If this disillusioned Britisher had travelled further, he might have learnt that the term Britisher is rarely heard in America; and that "the variety of railway gauges" does not as he alleges "necessitate constant changes of carriages," since there are about one hundred thousand miles of track of uniform gauge. There are more things he would have learnt had he stayed a few days longer. He might have acquired some of that good-nature which permits Americans to regard with equanimity even such gross misrepresentations of their country as his ungracious report.

It is no libel on one's own countrymen to say that
when abroad they are very eccentric. It is without
doubt a high distinction to be an Englishman—to feel
that the awe-struck foreigner is enviously thinking of
the glorious inheritance which has descended to his
grotesquely-attired person. But the grand traditions of
the race, the "glory of the empire," the dignity of the
Mother of Nations, are not enhanced by a swagger that
would provoke the derision of a street urchin if displayed in the Strand. "You take up a great deal of
room," was the remonstrance of an American to a
blustering Briton at a railway station. "I am accustomed to take up a great deal of room in my own
country," was the reply. "There can't be much room
left for others, then," smiled the Yankee. Sometimes,
however, we go to the opposite extreme ; as instance the
English lecturer—a man of high position at home—
who, having received an encouraging reply to his query,
"How much flattery can the Americans stand?" proceeded forthwith to disgust his friends and amuse his
audiences by insincere and servile adulation. I lately
saw a letter which this gentleman had written to a
newspaper, saying he had married an American lady
and that he was about to become a naturalized citizen!
To become a renegade is a queer way of flattering a
patriotic people.

Shrewdness, which is so marked a characteristic of
Americans, does not desert its possessor in presence of a
flatterer. When Archdeacon Farrar, at the Westminster
Abbey services, closed his eloquent tribute to General
Grant with a eulogy of the American people, a trans-
atlantic cousin was heard to say: "I'll lay odds he's

reckoning on a lecturing tour on the other side." And the guess turned out correct.

The peripatetic Briton who has visited America has left there innumerable stories of lost *h*'s. In a serial which appeared in *Lippincott's Magazine,* an earl is said to have delivered himself of the following: " It wasn't the 'unting that 'urt the 'orses, but the 'ammer, 'ammer, 'ammer on the 'ard 'ighroad!" This was possibly the gentleman I heard about at Montreal. A clerk at the Windsor Hotel there saw an Englishman opening doors on the hall floor in apparent search of something. " What are you looking for?" he asked. " I want an 'oister," said the son of Albion. " An oyster! You'll find plenty in the dining-room." " No, no," said the traveller with an impatient gesture; '' I want to go upstairs by the 'oister." " Oh, you want the elevator?" " Yes, the helevator!"

There is more reason for the American belief that every Englishman drops his *h*'s, than there is in the British tradition that all Americans speak through the nose, and use " tarnation" for an emphasis. The English of Americans is quite as good as that spoken at home; and the local differences are not nearly so great. The dialect of Lancashire, for example, has no parallel in America.   Amongst the cultured, great attention is paid to purity of speech, and though the accent is strange to English ears and the intonation monotonous, the grammar is generally faultless—if one except the very common solecism " it don't." Apropos of intonation, an American lady once told me she used to think that the English people she met displayed much affectation in their speech; and when she went to England she thought she had come to a nation of actors and actresses. And here we get the most important difference between our speech and the Americans': it is rather a difference of intonation than of language. To Americans the modulations of our voice are varied and musical; and I have frequently heard expressions of admiration when they have heard a soft-voiced Englishwoman. If Anglomaniacs were not so absurd in other respects, it would be a beneficial change if their imitation of the English voice could become common.

English writers on American affairs are rarely in favour on the other side, partly because of their ignorance of American subjects, partly because they are often unfair. They are unfair from prejudice, and their ignorance is sometimes due to the same cause, though occasionally one falls into blunders because things change so quickly in America. There is one English review that causes much mirth, and occasionally a little anger, by its mistakes. "Many of its accounts of what has happened or is going to happen," says a New York journalist, "are based, like General Choke's mode of proving that the Queen lives in the Tower of London, on notions of what ought naturally to happen." That there is ground for the American's assertion seems probable when we remember that a man of Mr. Matthew Arnold's standing ventured to write a little work, as he says, "on what I thought civilization in the United States might *probably* be like." A similar explanation might account for the curious fancies of a writer who lately discovered that "Aristocracy is not only legal in the United States, but it has been deliberately established in the constitution." According to this gentleman, who announced his discovery in the *Nineteenth Century Review,* the antagonism between the Com·

mons and the Lords in England is paralleled by a
contest between the American Senate and the House
of Representatives, the former body constituting a
menace to democracy as great as the hereditary English
chamber.   This is extremely funny.   The writer can
hardly be an American, though he dates from Chicago.
If he is, he is probably indulging in that form of Yankee
humour of which Englishmen rarely see the point.

One hears a great deal in England about the injustices
authors suffer through the absence of an international
copyright law with America.   But American authors
suffer from English pirates, too, though one hears little
of this form of criminal reciprocity.   Indeed our own
countrymen are the greatest offenders.   Like King
John, they set fire to the house they rob!   What I mean
will be seen from the following statement by the author
of "Ben Hur"—General Lew Wallace, late U. S. minister to Turkey:

"I found on reaching London about ten months ago," said
General Wallace, "that my novel of 'Ben Hur' was advertised
by Messrs. F. Warne & Co. as from their presses. They also advertise themselves as agents of *The Century* Company of this city,
and I find by looking at the magazine that they are so recognized
by the publishers here.   Of course I knew I had no legal rights
in England, but I was naturally curious to know something of the
style in which the book was reproduced in England, the character
of the house printing it and something about the success which it
had met with abroad.   So I called at their place and asked a
clerk if he had a novel called 'Ben Hur.'   He handed me a copy,
price two shillings, and I paid him for it.   I asked several questions which led naturally to the inquiry as to what sale the English edition had met with.   The clerk told me that they had sold
2000 copies in the past fortnight, a thousand a week.   That was
flattering, and I told him I was glad to hear it as I was the author.   'Indeed!' he exclaimed; and at the same moment he
reached out and took back the volume he had sold me.   He then

asked me if I would not remain where I was for a moment. He
disappeared and returned in a moment without my book, but with
a request that I would see the principals of the house. I was very
glad to do so, and going into the private office I met two gentlemen who were introduced to me as members of the firm. My
bought copy of my stolen book lay on the table, and I took it up
in the course of the conversation which followed and glanced at
it occasionally as we talked. At first the conversation was pleasant enough, but glancing at the title-page I found that the sub-title
had been changed from 'A Tale of the Christ' to 'The Days of
Christ.' That was annoying, and I asked who had authorized the
change. The reply was that the publishers had done it to avoid
hurting the sensibilities of religious readers in England. In other
words, they had appropriated my property and had changed it to
suit their own views of what its language and tone should be.
'Have you made any other of these unauthorized changes?' I
asked. 'Well, we have omitted two of the tales told by one of
the characters,' answered the speaker of the firm. You can imagine I was getting warmed up by this time and I spoke rather
strongly. But the next discovery enraged me beyond measure.
They had actually written up and inserted a preface to the novel.
No, not a publisher's preface. It was without signature of any
sort, and to the ordinary reader must have read as if by the author.
I had written no preface whatever. I demanded to know of them
what they proposed to do in the way of remunerating me for taking and for altering my book. They promised to give the matter
due consideration. That was ten months ago, and I have never
heard from them. I suppose they are taking plenty of time for
what they call 'due consideration.' The house is not a very important one outside of the fact that they are London agents of a
reputable American company."

This is but a mild sort of criminality compared with
some other cases known to me. A friend of mine wrote
a book of reference for children, which had a large sale
in America. Presently it appeared in England, "edited
by the Reverend Sir George W. Cox, Bart., M.A.," but
without any mention of the author. The "editing"

consisted in adding an article on an abstruse subject in
technical phraseology, and wholly unfit for children.
Later the plates passed into the hands of another publisher, who brought out a new edition. This time it
was not even "edited" by the Reverend Sir George W.
Cox, Bart., M.A.: it *was* by him! An American novel
was not long since adapted to English readers by the
substitution of the Queen for the President, and of the
Thames for the Connecticut! There is a thoroughness
about everything we English do!

Americans often return from Europe surprised and
chagrined at the ignorance of Englishmen concerning
things American. On one occasion when I crossed there
was a young fellow on board who had been an auction-
eer's clerk in London, and was going to settle in Minnesota. He was of average intelligence; but he was induced by some Americans to get out his gun before
reaching Sandy Hook, that he might have a shot at the
buffaloes which he was told would be seen browsing on

the seaweed of Brighton Beach. And a
young woman going out on the same
steamer to be married, declared that she
would not speak to her lover if he came
to meet her at the barge office dressed, as
she was told all Brooklynites dress at home,
in red flannel shirt, and slouch hat, trowsers tucked into top-boots, and pistols
showing prominently at the belt. At this
game of gulling the Englishman sometimes gets even with his tormentor. It

A Brooklynite!   is not long since a Yankee victim was
heard of inquiring the way to Abraham's Bosom, to
which an Englishman had recommended him as the

best club in London. Poor Harriet Martineau had many a hoax poured into her ear-trumpet, and some of them came out again in her book about America. And I fancy Henry Irving must have been victimized during his first trip. He wrote in the *Fortnightly Review :*

"In matter of duration [of theatrical performances], the audience is not to be trifled with or imposed on. I have heard of a case in a city of Colorado where the manager of a travelling company, on the last night of an engagement, in order to catch a through train, hurried the ordinary performance of his play into an hour and a half. When next the company were coming to the city they were met en route, some fifty miles out, by the sheriff, who warned them to pass on by some other way, as their coming was awaited by a large section of the able-bodied male population armed with shot-guns. The company did not, I am informed, on that occasion visit the city."

Every autumn brings its crop of stories of Englishmen's insatiable appetite for "gammon," exaggerated of course into that rhodomontade which is so important an element of American humour, but having, in many instances, a kernel of fact. It is not many years since an English novelist described a buffalo-hunt near Boston; and an English encyclopedia published not very long ago, had no knowledge of America's mineral deposits. Some years ago a young journalist with ambitions above his fellows, asked me to recommend him a special subject of study which was little known in England. I named "America;" and I was gratified that my advice was followed. He made a prolonged tour in America, and now in England he is making a successful career as a thoughtful and accurate writer on transatlantic affairs. It was he, by the way, who advised the immigrant who aspired to wealth to take up with a quack medicine until he had been long enough in the country

to make politics his profession. This happy conjunc-
tion of two very striking aspects of American life,
proves the efficiency of his studies of men and things in
the Republic!

English mistakes about America are made the more
absurd by the fact that our cousins are almost as familiar with England as are its inhabitants. Newspapers
devote nearly as much space to British public affairs as
to their own. Most educated Americans have travelled
in Europe; and everybody is familiar with recent English literature. The most popular plays are English,
and many actors and actresses have been educated with
us. But we are still dominated by the insular spirit—
the patriotic bias, as sociologists call it. It is said that
people born in Beacon Street, Boston, are regenerate
in the next world without being born again. At the bottom of the Briton's heart, there is some such faith in the
saving grace of his own nationality. That is why we
are always giving "points" to the nations—charging

them a good round
fee for the advice if
accepted, and bom-
barding their cities
or making naval dem-
onstrations against
them if rejected. I
see that certain
school-boards in Eng-
land are now feeding
children as well as
paying their school-
fees. The next
thing will be to send

them on foreign travels, thus utilizing the navy, and rubbing off that accumulation of hereditary conceit which causes the children of Albion to think, like the children of Israel, that the universe was created especially for their benefit, and that all Cosmos revolves round their little speck of earth.

The provincial spirit is found *à fortiori* in some Scotchmen. I have seen a letter from the editor of a Scottish paper published in New York, blaming a Scotchman for speaking of the inhabitants of Great Britain as Englishmen: he wanted them called Britons, forgetful that the population of Scotland is little greater than that of Lancashire, and not so great as that of London.

The Scotchman is a power in America. He is found everywhere—except in politics, which he leaves to his brother Celt from Ireland. Wherever found Sandy is usually at the head of things. It is predicted that he will be found at the top of the north pole when that is discovered. He is certainly at the top of the north pole of many a great manufacturing concern in America.

It does not take long to make a good American out of a Scotchman—if he is caught young. Dearly as he loves the land of brown heath and shaggy wood, he rarely wants to return to it. Dr. Johnson said that the prettiest sight in all Scotland was the road out of it. At the Burns dinner in New York, I heard many variations of this sentiment mixed with fervent love of the old country. One canny speaker referred to the tradition of the Scotchman's private ark at the Deluge, and hoped that his hearers had long since burnt this ark so that they could not get back to their beloved land—unless it be, said he, to mak' a visit. Our countrymen from

15

"ayont the Tweed" have made a splendid record in America. They have furnished much of the stuff that has made America great. Look at the array of Scotch names prominent in mercantile and financial circles of New York: Mackay, Morton, Murray, Mills, Grant, Stuart, Kennedy, Carnegie, Paton, Irvin, Henderson, Donald, Cameron, Ferguson, Macdonald, Reid, King, Maitland, Wallace, and a score of others. And all over the country similar lists could be found.

The predominance of English names in America is striking to one who has been impressed by the statistics of German and Scandinavian immigration. In a group of a score of native Americans, I counted the other day eighteen of distinct British origin; and one of the others was probably English. A book before me consisting of papers by seventeen writers—Harper's *First Century of the Republic*—does not contain a name that is positively un-English. Lists of Congressmen and Senators show a like preponderance; and there is hardly an honoured name in American history that is not English. The rotunda at Washington is full of statues of great Americans, every one of British stock. All the presidents and vice-presidents have been English—except perhaps Van Buren, and his first name was Martin. The long list of past judges of the Supreme Court contains but one foreign name. Mr. Bancroft estimates that during the first fifteen years of colonization, 21,200 persons, or 4000 families, arrived in New England. In 1840 the descendants of these, he estimates, amounted to four million—nearly one fourth of the whole population. Continuing the calculation, there would be at least eight million descendants of the earliest Puritan emigrants in 1870, and twelve million in 1885. Thus one person in every five in America is probably descended from the English who migrated to New England during the first fifteen years of colonization. This ratio would be greatly increased if we could estimate the numbers descended from the later colonists. German and other alien immigration is only of recent origin; and even now British immigrants are the most numerous. With few exceptions, relatively to their numbers, the American people are of pure English ancestry. They are in fact but star-spangled Britons. The exceptions are easily discovered. Even they, however, have been anglicized. German surnames have often English prefixes; and in many instances the name is translated. A German translator once said he had "overset" (übersetzt) the English. Many foreign names have been so overset, that their original form is no longer recognizable. Not in name only, but in nature, does the foreign element quickly become anglicized. The English language, literature and history are the joint heritage of the children of German immigrants and the descendants of the Puritans; and under their influence and that of the common school, the plastic youthful mind is soon moulded into harmony with its English environment.

When America broke away from the mother-country and started out for itself, its political loyalty was destroyed; but there has survived a higher sentiment—a loyalty to race traditions. As Englishmen at home are proud of the achievements of Englishmen beyond sea, so our transatlantic kindred share the greatness of our own branch of the race. They

love, of course, their own land best, just as we do; but after America, England. Americans share our pride in Shakspere, Milton, and that galaxy of poets and writers which has made our common language a richer storehouse than the tongues of any people, ancient or modern. Even in the nursery, the young American is soothed by an English lullaby, or charmed by the rhymes and stories of our own infancy. They sing to him a " Song o' Sixpence"—not of twelve cents; and Fe-fo-fum even in California smells "the blood of an Englishman" in preference to that of a Bostonian. The melody of their national anthem " My Country, 'tis of Thee"—is that of our own " God Save the Queen;" and " The Red, White and Blue"—is as familiar to Uncle Sam as it is to ourselves. Dear Dibdin's "Tom Bowling," heard in the Navy Yard at Annapolis or Washington, sounds as well as at Spithead or in the harbour at Malta. "Although his body's under hatches, his soul has gone aloft!"—gone aloft from many a ship with the Stars and Stripes at half-mast. Even at Cambridge they have a great seat of learning; and Yale and Harvard universities—light blue and dark blue— have their annual boat-race on the Thames. America is in truth *New* England. The history of old England is the history of Americans to within recent times. The halls and castles that moulder in the damp of England, live in pristine grandeur in transatlantic memories. Their names are revered and saved from oblivion by adoption. Our towns, where the pilgrim forefathers first drew breath, are kept green in the memory by transplantation of names. Boston or St. Biddulph's town in Lincolnshire, is still the acorn-hamlet it was two hundred and fifty years ago ; Boston, Massachusetts, its offspring, has become a city of world-wide renown, and a centre of intellectual activity which has made it the Alexandria of the New World. The name of Pendleton in the Blue Mountains of Oregon has doubtless a home-like ring to some wanderer from the banks of the Irwell. May the affection which crystallizes into forms so beautiful ever endure! May every loving thought borne on western breezes to " the old country," meet another on its way to some kinsman across the sea! May the community of blood, language, traditions and literature, be strengthened by a community of interests, which will bind mother and child more closely together than can political bonds ! Perhaps in the future, which gives such bright promise to the Greater Britain that has grown up beyond sea, Child and Mother-land shall stand together as of old—not in feudal dependency, but as leading states in the Federation of the World.

CHAPTER XVI.

A FRESH LOOK AT MANIFEST DESTINY.

" The future of the world belongs to us, to us who are of the same blood and language, if we are true to ourselves and to our opportunities, not of conquest or aggression, but of commercial development and beneficent influence."—*Gladstone.*

THE brilliant future of the American nation has probably furnished a text for more patriotic speeches than have ever been made outside the Republic. On this glowing topic the Fourth of July orator, ever since the Declaration of Independence, has annually got "inebriated with the exuberance of his own verbosity" and his country's resplendence. Here is an example which for patriotic braggadocio, is probably unparalleled even in America itself. It is a strain of exultation from distant Dakota:

" Where is all this gigantic growth and development to end? Will not the close of our century see all North America, from Behring's Strait to the Isthmus of Panama, under one glorious free government and tri-colored flag? Will not the mystical figures 'A.D. 1900' find us all, Canadians, United Statians, Mexicans, Guatemalans, and Nicaraguans, brethren and friends and fellow-citizens, marching beneath the starry banner of the free and the brave, to a grand common destiny of illimitable wealth and power and renown? Then shall Columbia's proud pet eagle (which is being so numerously and diversifiedly squeezed until he squawks to-day), perched upon the loftiest pinnacle-crag of the

royal-ore-ribbed Rocky Mountains, spread his cloud-bathed wings
from the multifloral rainbows and frost-wrought splendors of the
Aurora-Borealic realms, to where the billowed sunshine of Hondu-
rian gulfs chants its ceaseless anthem to shores of everlasting green
and gold, and trumpet forth in universe-reverberating tones his
' Cock-a-doodle-Yankee-doodle-doo ' of exultation and defiance to
all the world and the rest of mankind. Earth's two greatest
oceans, three thousand miles apart, shall roll up in thundering
oratorio their echo of the high and glad refrain; the mightiest
gulf and grandest lakes in all creation shall join the chant; river
after river, huge, rolling floods, shall conspire to swell the giant
pæans; Superior's waves, old Mississippi's torrent, Niagara's misty
thunders, shall roar it far and wide; the hurricane crashing
through ten thousand mountain gorges, from the Alleghanies to
the Cordilleras, from the Adirondacks to the Sierras, shall chime
it; the raging blizzards, hurling six-inch hailstones on sky-bounded
Nebraskan plains, shall whistle and rattle it; the catamount shall
shriek it, the prairie-wolf shall howl it, the lone owlet hoot it, and
the grizzly bear shall growl it; and the burden of it all shall be·
' America for Americans!   One country, one flag, zwei lager,
from Greenland's icy mountains to Darien's golden strands! E
pluribus unum, now, henceforth and forevermore, world without
end—amen!' "

This fervid Yankee obviously mistakes bulk for greatness.   Emerson somewhere says that the true test of
civilization is not the census, nor the size of cities, nor
the crops, but the kind of man the country produces.
Judged by this standard a large part of the superficial
area of the Republic, including the western home of the
orator just quoted, has hardly made such startling progress as to justify a universal *Lobgesang*. To many
western territories which surpass in area the most
civilized countries of the old world, Bishop Heber's
description of Ceylon and the Ceylonese might be aptly
applied.

Stripped of its bombast there is, however, much in

the national progress of which America may justly feel proud. In material wealth and population her advance is marvellous. Ten years of progress in America equal twenty years in England, and half a century in some other parts of Europe. The wealth of the United States has quadrupled in less than thirty years, and multiplied sixteen-fold in the memory of persons living. As Mulhall shows in his "Balance-sheet of the World," the increase of Uncle Sam's wealth since 1850 would suffice to buy up the German empire, with its farms, cities, banks, shipping, manufactures, Krupp guns and millions of conscripts. The annual accumulation has been 165 million sterling; and therefore each decade adds more to the wealth of the United States than the capital value of Italy or Spain! Each year witnesses the birth of towns which in less than a decade surpass in size, wealth and material comforts many old-world cities whose names are found on every page of history. Geneva is only half the size of Milwaukee; Cleveland is as large as Genoa; Duluth, a fifteen-year-old city, exceeds Mecca or Jerusalem in population; Venice is not as big as Detroit, and Rome is only half the size of Chicago. Though many persons may consider such comparisons fanciful and absurd, it is probable that these young flourishing cities of America are destined to exercise as great an influence on the history of the world, as any of the ancient cities have done. Their power as cities may not be so great; their influence may be but that of coöperating units; but they are units of a magnificent Whole, which is working out a revolution in political and industrial methods more comprehensive than anything that has preceded it in time.

Any forecast concerning America which goes further

forward than ten or twenty years must seem chimerical to many people. How would John Adams or Benjamin Franklin or George Washington have received a prophecy which gave a full and clear account of the United States in the year 1887: the population swollen to twelve times the number they knew; the mile-a-minute trains that would cross the then unexplored continent in a few days; the material wealth greater than all the world had seen before; the six days' sail to Europe in mammoth steamships of palatial luxury; the British House of Lords rising to honour the American minister; and a funeral oration on an ex-president within sound of André's monument in Westminster Abbey! The condition of America in the year 1987 would appear equally visionary if described to us to-day. Let us not look so far ahead.

The population of America has repeatedly doubled itself in twenty-five years. The census of 1880, however, showed that the population was several millions short of being double that of 1855, or four times that of 1830. Probably it will never again double itself in so short a time. Taking thirty years or even more as the period required, it is safe to say that during the lives of persons now living, the Republic will count two hundred million citizens. Even with this enormous population, America will be five times less densely peopled than the United Kingdom is now. If ever America becomes as thickly peopled as England, the population will number 1,785,000,000!

It is unquestionably the " manifest destiny " of America to leave all the nations of the world far behind. She has already a greater population than any European nation except Russia; and no people increase so rapidly.

France has taken one hundred and sixty years to double her population, and now she appears to be declining. Great Britain multiplies faster than any other European people; yet she has taken seventy years to double her number—nearly three times as long as America. In half a century, indeed, America has *added* to her numbers more than the present population of Great Britain, of France, or of Austria!

Equally marvellous has been her progress in manufactures. In ten years the aggregate of industries rose thirty-five per cent. The actual increase, as stated by Mulhall, was 525 million sterling, against 337 million of Great Britain. In 1870, American-made steel was less than one fourth the quantity made in Germany, and less than half that made in France. Ten years later—only ten years—she made more than France, Germany, Austria and Belgium combined! Progress is a word which fails to express such an expansion! The manufactures of America now exceed in value those of any other nation—even of England, which has hitherto led the world. In agriculture, of course, she is without a rival.

And our own branch of the English race—what are its industrial achievements? In manufactures we still lead the old world in a way that admits of no comparison. Our textile industries have trebled in value in fifty years, and our yearly product is two sevenths of the world's output. Our cotton industry has trebled in thirty years; and while our product is double that of the United States, it is nearly four times as great as that of any other country, and is more than one third of the product of the world. The spindles of the United Kingdom are nearly half the total of the world. Of steel we make as much as all the rest of Europe put together; and half as much again of iron. More than one third of the commerce of the world is ours. In forty-five years it bounded from 95 million sterling to 570 million sterling. We have acquired more than half the carrying trade of the world; and five ships in ten the world over fly the union jack. Our tonnage nearly doubled between 1870 and 1880; and between 1876 and 1885, the increased tonnage of British steamships was two million tons—an addition equal to twice the entire tonnage of the French mercantile navy, after including such small fry as fishing-smacks, pilot-boats, and vessels lying ashore!

During the present century the English in America have added to their territory more than three million square miles—twice the area of our Indian Empire, which supports a population of 250 million. The English at home have done more. They have taken possession of all the choicest parts of the world; so that other nations, ambitious to found colonies, have now to take jungles and swamps in the torrid zone. The British Empire contains nine million square miles—one fifth of the habitable globe. Every nationality under the sun is represented in this mighty Empire; yet there is nowhere a single English-speaking community under foreign rule. These sixty-five dependencies have for the most part their own governments elected by the people. Each is therefore a stronghold of democracy. In New Zealand even the native Maoris vote, and they have elected five of their race to the House of Representatives. Stated briefly, the English race is in possession of one third of the habitable world; under its rule lives one fourth of the human race; its governments are everywhere controlled by the people—for even the government of India is subordinate to the democracy at home. In brief, our race is supreme in industry, in trade, in agriculture. It is by far the most numerous of civilized races; it is also the wealthiest; and what is more important, the richest in character. It is dominant in the thought of mankind; in political methods it is greatly in advance of other peoples. In everything which makes a people great, the supremacy of the English race is the most prominent fact of this age.

It is in no spirit of vain-glory that I reiterate these tokens of English greatness; although I consider them a cause for legitimate pride. It is of implications that I would speak. These facts are pregnant with a meaning which every year's growth of America and England makes clearer. They indicate the ultimate predomi- nance of the English race, with the corollary that our language will be the speech of the world. "Will be," say I? It is already. Not long ago the native representatives of China and Japan, during negotiations at Tientsin concerning the affairs of Corea, conducted their discussions in the English tongue.* Already English is the native language of a hundred million people—five times as many as at the beginning of this century. At present our language is spoken by nearly two sevenths of the civilized world. In 1801 thirteen Europeans in every hundred spoke English, while about twenty spoke French, which was of all Euro- pean languages the most used. Now there are but

---

* Since writing this an American friend from China assures me that at this conference, the contribution of the Japanese representa- tive to the discussion was the single expression *My hop pacific.* The hope for peace concealed in the phrase is decidedly encourag- ing. May every extension of our language be accompanied by a hop pacific!

thirteen French in every hundred to more than twenty-seven English.

At the close of the civil war in America—which has so far lost its bitterness that it has come to be spoken of simply as "the late unpleasantness"—Napoleon was in Mexico. He was there, as he himself said, to assure by means of French soldiers "the preponderance of France over the Latin races, and to augment the influence of these races in America." As soon as Uncle Sam had put his house in order, he hinted to Napoleon that Mexico was part of America, and came within the operation of that law formulated by Monroe. The French took the hint and left. Mexico has a share in the manifest destiny of the Republic which a keener man than Napoleon recognized. Thirty-five years ago Lucan Alaman, the Mexican statesman and historian, left on record the pathetic prophecy that the future greatness of his country would "not be for the races which now inhabit it." Since then the destiny of Mexico has become more manifest. Her rich valleys and mines have tempted southwards thousands of rich Americans, who are developing the latent powers of the country. It will not be long before Mexico drops into the starry group of States. From Mexico it is only a step to Central America, where there will soon be a ship railway of primary importance to the Republic. America's authority has already been asserted and acknowledged in Panama. The manifest destiny of the Republic certainly includes Mexico and Central America. Then, still looking south, it seems impossible that the vast regions included in the name of South America can remain in the possession of the emasculated Europeans and Latinized half-breeds who now live there. England already has a foothold there; great possibilities lie in the future. Americans say of an unreasonable man that he wants the earth. Without consciously wanting it, it seems probable that the English race will get it. There is only one continent left for other nations to wrangle over; and even of this we have picked out for ourselves the choicest bits. The northern boundary of the British possessions in South Africa now almost reaches the Zambesi. It is barely a generation since this river was practically unknown.

Here let me quote a paragraph from Prof. Fiske's little book on *American Political Ideas.* It is especially interesting to our branch of the English race, as expressing the belief of an American in our common "manifest destiny."

"The work which the English race began when it colonized North America is destined to go on until every land on the earth's surface that is not already the seat of an old civilization *shall become English in its language, in its political habits and traditions, and to a predominant extent in the blood of its people.* The day is at hand when *four fifths of the human race will trace its pedigree to English forefathers,* as four fifths of the white people in the United States trace their pedigree to-day. The race thus spread over both hemispheres, and from the rising to the setting sun, will not fail to keep that sovereignty of the sea and that commercial supremacy which it began to acquire when England first stretched its arm across the Atlantic to the shores of Virginia and Massachusetts. The language spoken by these great communities will not be sundered into dialects like the language of the ancient Romans, but perpetual intercommunication and the universal habit of reading and writing will preserve its integrity; and the world's business will be transacted by English-speaking people to so great an extent, that whatever language any man may have learned in his infancy, he will find it necessary sooner or later to express his thoughts in English. And in this way it is by no means improbable that, as Grimm the German and Candolle the Frenchman long since foretold, the language of Shakespeare may ultimately become the language of mankind."

Returning to our Arithmancy, let us look at shadows cast by some events which are not so remote. The most conspicuous augury is that American industry, free from the most oppressive burdens which feudalism has bequeathed to other nations, will outstrip European industry just as America is outdistancing everything else European. Then in sheer self-defence, the warlike nations of the Old World will have to drop militancy as a pastime too expensive when starving for food. Perhaps the burden of hereditary privilege will be dropped at the same time. The first king was only a leader in war : with cessation of war, royalty becomes not only useless, but detrimental as a profitless burden on industry.

America is fast becoming the market-garden and provision store-house of Europe. Her shipments of food are already indispensable to the Old World ; and Europe's dependence on the Republic will increase. Europe must give something in exchange for cargoes of wheat, beef, pork, etc. What will she give when America not only becomes self-sufficing, but sends her cheap manufactures into the neutral markets of the world? Already her exports are 31 per cent in excess of imports. This problem will get more difficult of solution as it grows old. America, favoured by great natural resources, and untrammelled by military taxation or service, free from war debts and from the burden of royalty and large classes of non-producers, will soon undersell the products of Europe in every market. This is the way in which the Western Republic will join the European concert. Her entry will produce greater changes in governmental theory and methods than the advent of a political Wagner or a Berlioz. It may be visionary to speculate how the other musicians will receive such an advent. To me only one result seems possible : Europe will have to send her sons home from the barrack and camp, that in the forge and workshop they may take part in a struggle keener than that of Waterloo. The contest will be industrial. Shuttles, picks and hammers will be the weapons. The victory, like that of military encounters, will be survival to the fittest ; but the fittest here is the one possessing the most efficient and economical industrial system.

It is a doubtful question, however, whether the peoples of Europe will be content to wait until the industrial contest between themselves and America becomes so keen as that described. To the most unobservant person it must be growing clear that destructive forces of unparalleled magnitude are rapidly accumulating under the political systems of Europe. If the process continues, there must ere long come a crash that will hurl the last remnants of feudalism from the world. Russian Nihilism, like a horrible catacomb of skulls and

dead men's bones, forms a subterranean system which
undermines the empire ; and the eyes of the world are
turned, half in hope, in daily expectation of the crash.
Germany, with her hordes of socialists and hundreds of
thousands of discontented conscripts, is hardly more
stable in her political foundations than her northern
neighbour. France is perpetually simmering with excitement, and no prediction can say on which side she
will next boil over, perhaps bringing about the universal
ebullition that has been so long preparing. In Spain
plots are rife to overthrow the monarchy and establish
a republic. In Austria a demand has arisen for a
Zollverein with Germany, which statesmen oppose.
England has armies of hungry men parading the streets,
demanding work ; agitations for the abolition of the
lords are becoming more vehement and more frequent ;
the demands of royalty are received with growing sul-
lenness ; and in Ireland we have a province almost in
rebellion. Turkey is toppling over, and threatens soon

"Let there be Light !"

to fall "bag and baggage" out of
Europe. Everywhere is unrest. Millions of armed men cannot prevent discontent among people who are beginning to learn that every honest man
is politically as good as any other man.
"The divine right of kings to govern
wrong" is being confronted by the divine right of the people to govern
themselves. The divinity that did
hedge a king, *now hedges him in*. The knell of kings
and nobles was rung a hundred years ago by the cracked
bell which now hangs mute in the old Liberty Hall
at Philadelphia ; and its reverberations have not ceased

16

to be heard in Europe. Did Victor Hugo not speak aright when he said, "It is the third gate of Barbarism —the monarchical gate—which is closing at this moment. The Nineteenth Century hears it rolling on its hinges."

Some time ago a democratic pæan in an English newspaper was flashed across the Atlantic, to show the sympathizing Republic how sentiment is tending to complete democracy in the old country. The occasion was the quiet return to private life of the late President of the United States, and the inauguration of his successor. Here is a ringing verse from the pæan:

"Hear this, ye kings with your tawdry crowns, ye dukes and earls with your tinsel coronets, ye Lords of the Bedchamber and Gold Sticks in Waiting with your salaries drawn from the hard-earned wages and slender resources of the thrifty poor—salaries paid to you for no service productive of good to the public, but only for playing the flunky and the fool! Is it not time, O patient English democracy, for us to open our eyes and take counsel of our wiser children? The money wasted over the pomp and pageantry of courts is spent in bolstering up the pretensions of rank and birth. Would it not be better spent in feeding the poor and teaching the ignorant?"

Exit earl!

Every European who works for his bread, and by his labour contributes to maintain the hereditary drones of his nation, will sympathize in heart with this outburst. He may doubt whether the present be an opportune moment for throwing off the incubus; but it is clear to him as noonday, if he is keeping pace with the age, that a tremendous change is needful and imminent. The labourers of Europe are terribly overtasked; and in competition with the industrial system of the Western Republic, the pressure is soon to become insupportable.

There is one aspect of this question of special interest to Englishmen—an aspect often overlooked by royalists and republicans at home and abroad. " The men who make kings are not subjects," said the French chamber of Louis Philippe. So too we Englishmen, who can end the monarchy in three hours by repealing the Act of Settlement, cannot logically be classed as subjects. If any one is a subject in England, it is surely the monarch, who is subject to the will of the people. Even the President of the Republic cannot be displaced by the people as promptly as can our own monarch.

John Bright, " England's greatest Commoner and America's staunchest friend," whose name is revered in every home on both sides of the Atlantic, lately said: " I am satisfied that if it were possible for England and France and Germany and Austria and Russia and Italy to abolish the tariffs and let commerce flow freely, it would be beyond the possibility of King or Queen or Czar or Kaiser or Statesmen of any rank to bring those nations to war."

If the industrial capacities of Europe are tried in competition with America to the extent expected, free trade will become absolutely imperative. The federation of the nations of Europe will then follow as " the night the day"—or more correctly, as the day the night. Come, happy day! Mankind has suffered long and silently. Let feudalism follow slavery!

Though this end may be too remote to have any immediate interest for the passing generation, those who believe in the ultimate triumph of democracy over privilege and legalized wrong, who cherish the thought that industrialism is destined to conquer militancy, that feudalism must ultimately give way to federalism, can rejoice that the tendencies of the age are towards the emancipation of the race, once and forever.   To hasten on this change is America's "manifest destiny"—maybe, by such prosaic means as underselling Europe in the world's markets.   Her statue of Liberty enlightening the World is more than a gigantic toy: it is the symbol of her mission to mankind.   She has a nobler function among

"And there was Light!"

nations than the invention of labour-saving machines or caterer of provisions.   She stands a living example to the suffering democracies of the old world.   Liberty is enlightening the World.   Attempts to arrest its influence will be as vain as Canute's imperious command to the tide.   Those who believe in the everlasting principle of Progress may hear without dismay the trumpet-blast

> " That shakes old systems with a thunder-fit.
>   The time is ripe, and rotten ripe, for change;
>   Then let it come: I have no dread of what
>   Is called for by the instinct of mankind."

THE END.

Foreign Travelers in America
1810–1935

AN ARNO PRESS COLLECTION

Archer, William. **America To-Day**: Observations and Reflections. 1899.

Belloc, Hilaire. **The Contrast**. 1924.

[Boardman, James]. **America, and the Americans**. By a Citizen of the World. 1833.

Bose, Sudhindra. **Fifteen Years in America**. 1920.

Bretherton, C. H. **Midas, Or, The United States and the Future**. 1926.

Bridge, James Howard (Harold Brydges). **Uncle Sam at Home**. 1888.

Brown, Elijah (Alan Raleigh). **The Real America**. 1913.

Combe, George. **Notes on the United States Of North America During a Phrenological Visit in 1838-9-40**. 1841. 2 volumes in one.

D'Estournelles de Constant, Paul H. B. **America and Her Problems**. 1915.

Duhamel, Georges. **America the Menace**: Scenes from the Life of the Future. Translated by Charles Miner Thompson. 1931.

Feiler, Arthur. **America Seen Through German Eyes**. Translated by Margaret Leland Goldsmith. 1928.

Fidler, Isaac. **Observations on Professions, Literature, Manners, and Emigration, in the United States and Canada, Made During a Residence There in 1832**. 1833.

Fitzgerald, William G. (Ignatius Phayre). **Can America Last?** A Survey of the Emigrant Empire from the Wilderness to World-Power Together With Its Claim to "Sovereignty" in the Western Hemisphere from Pole to Pole. 1933.

Gibbs, Philip. **People of Destiny**: Americans As I Saw Them at Home and Abroad. 1920.

Graham, Stephen. **With Poor Immigrants to America**. 1914.

Griffin, Lepel Henry. **The Great Republic**. 1884.

Hall, Basil. **Travels in North America in the Years 1827 and 1828**. 1829. 3 volumes in one.

Hannay, James Owen (George A. Birmingham). **From Dublin to Chicago**: Some Notes on a Tour in America. 1914.

Hardy, Mary (McDowell) Duffus. **Through Cities and Prairie Lands:** Sketches of an American Tour. 1881.

Holmes, Isaac. **An Account of the United States of America,** Derived from Actual Observation, During a Residence of Four Years in That Républic, Including Original Communications. [1823].

Ilf, Ilya and Eugene Petrov. **Little Golden America:** Two Famous Soviet Humorists Survey These United States. Translated by Charles Malamuth. 1937.

Kerr, Lennox. **Back Door Guest.** 1930.

Kipling, Rudyard. **American Notes.** 1899.

Leng, John. **America in 1876:** Pencillings During a Tour in the Centennial Year, With a Chapter on the Aspects of American Life. 1877.

Longworth, Maria Theresa (Yelverton). **Teresina in America.** 1875. 2 volumes in one.

Low, A[lfred] Maurice. **America at Home.** [1908].

Marshall, W[alter] G[ore]. **Through America:** Or, Nine Months in the United States. 1881.

Mitchell, Ronald Elwy. **America:** A Practical Handbook. 1935.

Moehring, Eugene P. **Urban America and the Foreign Traveler, 1815-1855.** With Selected Documents on 19th-Century American Cities. 1974.

Muir, Ramsay. **America the Golden:** An Englishman's Notes and Comparisons. 1927.

Price, M[organ] Philips. **America After Sixty Years:** The Travel Diaries of Two Generations of Englishmen. 1936.

Sala, George Augustus. **America Revisited:** From the Bay of New York to the Gulf of Mexico and from Lake Michigan to the Pacific. 1883. 3rd edition. 2 volumes in one.

Saunders, William. **Through the Light Continent;** Or, the United States in 1877-8. 1879. 2nd edition.

Smith, Frederick [Edwin] (Lord Birkenhead). **My American Visit.** 1918.

Stuart, James. **Three Years in North America.** 1833. 2 volumes in one.

Teeling, William. **American Stew.** 1933.

Vivian, H. Hussey. **Notes of a Tour in America from August 7th to November 17th, 1877.** 1878.

Wagner, Charles. **My Impressions of America.** Translated by Mary Louise Hendee. 1906.

Wells, H. G. **The Future in America:** A Search After Realities. 1906.